In These St... S0-AGL-990

Written by: Empress Simone

Copyright @2015 Empress Simone

Published by: Empressed For Life Presents

Facebook: Author Empress Simone

Instagram: EmpressSimone1

This novel is a work of Fiction. Any resemblances to actual events, real people, living or dead, organizations, locales or establishments are products of the Author's imagination. Other names, characters, places and incidents are used fictiously.

Cover Design Art by: Angel Walker

Acknowledgements

I would like to say Thank you to Our Lord and Savior Jesus Christ who strengthens us to do all things.

Thank you to My Parents, Adrian and Rachel, for the guidance and correction you have always given to me.

Thank you to my three Beautiful mini ME's, Desiree, Dominique and Donovan, my children and my heart. I wish you well in all your endeavors.

Thank you to Angel Walker, for the wonderful cover art.

To all my wonderful literary sisters and brothers for the encouragement and guidance given me during my journey on becoming an author.

A special thank you goes out to my sharing circle(s) Toni McKoy, Candace Mumford, Lynice Jackson, Angel Bearfield, Sentu Taylor, Anjela Day, Midnite Love, Cha'Bella Don, Deidra Daniel, Honey Bee, London Starr and Fatima Munroe.

To my loving family, which are entirely too many relatives to mention by name. I love you all and thank you all for the roles you have played in my life.

As always, I wish to give a shout out to all my supporters and avid readers. I truly am grateful to you all and I admire you for giving a new Author encouragement, support and yes constructive criticism. #YouRock.

Dedications

As always, this book is dedicated to the wonderful and loving memory of my Grandmother Nina, who is my Angel, and Queen. I adore you and miss you so much mere words can't explain. I am and will always be unapologetic in my love and admiration of you.

To my Grandmother Marie Bell and my aunt Patsy Olds, I love you and miss you both very much.

My friend Doris Vega and baby boy Jamell, domestic violence is never okay. He took away good people when he took you both from us. Rest in Paradise my friend(s).

Chapter 1

Shatease was my right hand. I guess you could call
her my rider. We were what everyone referred to as
Day 1's. We always had each other's back. If I wasn't
at home watching my younger siblings and my older
non-verbal autistic brother, then I was at her house
and vice versa. Her mother and mine were road dogs.
Any illegal activities they were bound together by
actions. The two were even co-defendants in more
than a few cases. They hardly served any time only
community service and ACD's. I remember having to
do the verification of my mother's identity once or
twice. This is where an officer would call the home
and ask if I knew Angela Bettenfield? What was her
date of birth and how long she lived at the current
address? One officer even asked if she worked or
went to school. The idea seemed so foreign to me. I
replied by screaming, "hell no," then hung up the
phone.

Shatease and I didn't like to admit to anyone but each
other, how deep our mothers were afflicted by drug
use. They were full blown crack heads. Their habits
went further than recreational use.

As we became older we were able to decipher the
depth of their habits. It seemed nothing was
farfetched in the attempts they made to get high.

[5]

Especially, when the clothes Shatease and I boosted started to go missing, the video games we bought for ourselves and siblings disappeared and the High Def. flat screen TV went missing. They usually would stroll in hours later, eyes jumping, scratching their skin looking for more valuables to sell for their elicit pleasures.

Shatease and my dude Griff were my only escape from a cruel world. This world was known to many as the MacDougal family. I am called Koi. My real name is Eliza Ma' Koi MacDougal. I am named after one of my enslaved ancestors. I believe it was their spirit which drove me in most of my actions. I was a strong fighter in every sense of the word.

I always thought on the events which caused my mother to start getting high. Truth be known at one time she was an outstanding citizen. It seemed her world shattered when my father Shaleeq MacDougal was murdered. I was age five and remember it like it was yesterday. Seem like good ole Shaleeq was into number running, prostitution and minor gun running. He double crossed a major boss and a hit was put out for him. The one time my mother discussed my father's ill fate she said he needed the extra money as a come up. His thought pattern told him he could be his own boss. She was pregnant again at the time and already had three children. The meager allotment his boss paid him was barely enough to cover the rent. Shoes, clothes and food were needed as well.

Instead of bringing the money, guns and drugs back from an out of state run from Arkansas, he showed up to the drop off at the boss's place with no product, guns or money and a little roughed up. My mother said it was a job his partner Louis did so he didn't hurt him too badly. The boss took one look at him and it was the beginning of the end for my father.

Shaleeq MacDougal was murdered coming from church with my mother, my two year old sister and my brother who was in her belly. I, of course, was the one holding my father's hand and as always my older brother was walking ever so slowly behind all of us... His brain and skull fragments were blown onto the side of my face. I still remember my initial shock and amazement. My mother's soul piercing scream and my older brother Junior screaming still haunted me in my dreams. Junior's scream was an awkward sound. It was as if a ten month old, in a seven year old boy's body, was saying, 'Da-da', for the first time. My father's body hit the concrete with a thud and one eye ball hung out the socket. My mother let go of my two year old sister's hand and pushed me so hard I flew a couple of paces back. She dropped to her knees and screamed, "Leeq, get up! Leeq, don't do this baby! I need you! We all need you!"

I was frozen in time for a moment as I took in the gunman's demeanor. He really stuck around to make sure the job was done. He didn't budge from the corner until my father's body was on the floor and the family was huddled around him. He looked at me then started to take his face mask off. It was one of those 'Set it Off' mask from the restaurant scene. It only had a slight variation. From the bottom half of his face, all I saw was a smirk. His partner touched his arm and shook his head no. They then raced off and ran up the train steps to the platform. Surveillance cameras later showed they crossed the tracks and caught the train heading in the opposite direction. My family was never the same after that and my mother began her downward crack spiral.

I was good at a few things other than fighting. Dancing was on the list as well as math. Since I was a little girl I remember thinking I would become a ballerina. Then project life hit me, Mitchell projects in the South Bronx was anything but nice. I began to cut school and hang out in the hallways and exits with the other thugs. Some parents worked and some slept all day recuperating from all night drug binges. Anyway you looked at it, we children, were on our own. I swear out of the school year we only made it there the first day. In rare instances, sometimes we made it to school once a month. However, it wasn't our priority.

I held the drug packages for the young local dealers. In doing so I was able to put my math skills to use when it came to counting the money and how much change they had to give back to an addict. After a while, a friend put me on to boosting and how to pop the tags so the alarm couldn't go off. Some stores were smart and had better anti-theft systems than others. For those stores we made 'hot bags' so the alarms wouldn't ring and bust us. 'Hot bags' were just big shopping bags laced with aluminum foil in the inside. The aluminum blocked out whatever signal the tags would send off.

Sometimes we would 'borrow' the local addict's baby, providing, if they were in a stroller. We would then put the bags at the bottom of the stroller and then casually stroll through the store looking at the high priced items. When we found items that interested us we would throw them in the 'hot bag' at the bottom of the stroller. If we had received an order from the local drug dealers 'wifey' her order came first before our own needs. They spent the most money and gave us big tips. It was only right they received special treatment.

There were times though where things didn't go smoothly. Once or twice I had to smack a dealer's wifey up for thinking I was her personal assistant. Some would act all high siddity and start getting beside herself. I was young but not with any childish games. Name calling and trying to lay hands on me was not accepted. I remember the altercation I had with Nakisha in particular. She was Griff's main chick out of many. She was a little flippant because I brought her a navy blue form fitting halter top dress instead of a black flowing number. I told her I knew it was important for her to have a nice dress for the cruise Griff was taking her on. I overheard how he was going all out for their one year anniversary. He arranged for a Hot 97 deejay to host a party boat. The boat was to cruise the murky New York waters. Griff set aside a portion of the boat to be V.I.P with bottle service, a camera man with scenery in the background plus a videographer. Every boat ride occupant in attendance would receive a complimentary glass of champagne and a dinner plate. The dinner plates consisted of Barbecue chicken (grilled on board), yellow rice and asparagus. My dude Griff went all out for this occasion.

Nakisha must have lost her mind and thought I was her child because she started cursing at me. "Bitch, I told you a black dress. I don't care about importance. I want what I want. My shoes are silver, now how the hell silver shoes going to go with a navy dress. I think once you calm down, you will see that the silver matches the navy just fine. Matter of fact the navy look better than all the black dresses I saw that day. Accessorize with all sterling silver jewelry and you should have no problem."

Next thing I know a glob of spit was hitting my eye. That was the nastiest thing anyone could have ever done to me. I gave her two good pops in the same eye and then an upper cut to the body area. Nakisha went tumbling backwards. Nakisha banged into the wall hard. She slid down and started whooping and hollering. She went to saying how she never did anything to me but try and be my friend. She couldn't understand how I could hit her that way for no reason. That she was going to fuck me up when she got her bearings. I laughed at her, feeling she wasn't in a position to make terroristic threats. She went on for a couple of minutes.

Hearing enough I took one step towards her and she threw her arms over her head in an attempt to stop me from doing even more damage. I looked at the bitch and wanted to give her an Oscar for her performance. Griff, who saw the whole thing, jumped up from his fluorescent orange sofa and grabbed me, "What the fuck you doing Koi? You didn't have to hit her like that."

He grabbed me around my waist and started walking me out the door. Out in the hallway he stated, "Way to go Tiger. That's some nasty ass shit. I would have blown her motherfucking brains out her head for that one."

Griff patted me on the ass and rubbed in between my thighs. I reached out and grabbed his dick through his pants. I began to rub his package. He started saying things I desperately wanted to hear from him, "You know I am happy you are mines." My personal favorite was, "You better not give my pussy away."

I looked at him sideways and all I could muster was, "hmm, hmm." I figured he didn't want to be denied the sexual intimacy tonight or something. He gave me one hundred and fifty dollars. The fifty was a tip on top of the fee for the dress.

Later on that night, I saw Nakisha and Griff headed out. He wound up getting some black slacks with an electric blue button down shirt, some silver cuff links and silver gator shoes. I guess he was trying to make her feel good by color coordinating with her outfit. From the whistles I heard from the local thugs and the smile on Nakisha's face from the attention, it wasn't hard to tell I made the right decision. Too bad she didn't realize it before the spit hit my eye because she wound up looking just a tad bit clownish with the extra make up she had to put on the bruise under her eye.

I spent all night hustling with the boys who were a fixture every late night in front of the building. Thoughts of Griff ran through my head that night but I pushed them to the back of my mind. I was too young to be with him. Well, that is what he told me when I begged him for more than the occasional encounters in the hallway exits. Griff had a magical way of rubbing my titties and sucking them while finger popping me. I was still a 'virgin' technically as I had yet to be penetrated by anyone. I was praying silently Griff would change that for me.

Being innocent looking, I pulled the wool over most people eyes. Standing at a mere 5'4, I was dark brown skinned with a nice clear complexion, no pimples and no blemishes. I was a little thin but had an advantage over most females my age because I started to develop breast early. However, I was America's nightmare, Young, Black and Angry. People soon found out either they gave me what I wanted or I was taking it, even though I was small my hands were lethal. As a result, I soon received a reputation as a fighter, one who was short fused and liable to cut you if I was losing. If you met my extended family, especially my aunties, you would know why I was so rough. Shatease was a little mellower than I but she still would punch a bitch in the eye. Because of my aunties I was as tough as nails. They were all strong women who didn't tolerate disrespect of any kind.

As children, my siblings, cousins and myself, were told if one wanted to fight us or bully us we were to hold our own. There weren't any circumstances we should run home crying. If that happened my aunties would spank our tail and make us fight again. It didn't matter how big or small my opponent was, if they were Black, white or Latino. Fighting does not recognize color, borough or accent. The only thing it recognizes is respect. It was that sentiment drilled home to us at all times. My own mother used to say, "Who do you want to fight; them or me?" The smart ones in my family always choose them. Trust and believe if you were messing with any one of my

siblings the consequences were worse. I was
definitely going to draw blood out my opponent's ass.

My cousins weren't any picnic either. I could blame
them for my temperament as well. I swear I shudder
every time I think of them. They would treat me
unfairly. My cousins were always tagging my small
ass for some reason. If I tried to tell an adult they
would stuff my mouth with dirty socks and slap me in
the face with a hand full of Vaseline. It was horrible
at times but not all bad. I remember the shared
Christmases and Thanksgiving dinners. Our heads
bowed in prayers, the laughter as we passed the gravy
or mashed potatoes, summer days of jumping double
dutch or running through the fire hydrants or even a
simple game of flag football.

If my mother's boosting friends could steal enough
outfits, with shoes to match, we celebrated Easter as
well. Easter was one of the few holidays all heathens
and saints congregated together. I guess they were all
just putting on a fashion show of sorts. Afterwards,
whoever child looked a hot ass mess was talked about
to all high heavens.

Most of the time, my mother made sure to have us an
outfit with our hair freshly braided, beads at the end
and aluminum foil at the tips or we all stayed in the
house for a couple of days. Her favorite line, if she
thought anyone was being disrespectful talking about
us, "I'd hate to stomp a mud hole in a hoe out here

today for talking about mine. Ya hear me?" We all would look at each other wide eyed then back to her, "Yes ma'am," we all stated in unison. My momma was no joke with them hands either.

Sadly, one time Shatease and I had to double team our own crack headed mommas. By no means did I feel sorry for them. The pair were devious and on one Christmas sold my younger siblings presents. The deed was so unforgivable Shatease and I laid hands on them.

Shatease momma received the worse of our doubled rage during one of our royal rumbles. I released the fist of fury on her first. Shatease jumped in when I slipped. I landed in an awkward position on my back. Shatease mother tried to take full advantage of the situation and swooped in for the kill. However, my rider caught her with a swift knee to the midsection while I hurriedly scrambled to my feet.

Shatease better had thanked God she came to my rescue. It was only right since I was fighting for her two year old daughter's decency. Shatease had her at the tender age of thirteen. Her daughter's father was a white, adult limousine driver. He messed with the Hood rats' for recreation. He would pay them money for sexual services. Shatease said it was only one time that went too far. She said that although things were getting hot and heavy she insistently told him no when his penis tip hit her vagina. She stopped short of calling it rape but did say he kept going despite her saying no. It was this instance she became pregnant. He denied the child at first because of his wife. Shatease would lie to welfare about her child father's real name. This was done in an attempt to keep the authorities out of the situation.

Joshua Cravy finally came to his senses. For her helping him elude any back lash or charges from authorities or welfare petitioning him for a child support order through family court, he gave her large sums of money every month. Well, larger than what she was used to getting from anyone. Sha-Sha said the monetary support totaled more than five hundred dollars. However, during one argument I overheard her tell him, "Three hundred dollars don't go far when you have a family that milks you for everything you got anyway."

I hated to pry but a white guy who drove a limousine probably could afford more than three hundred dollars, especially if he stopped tricking on every hoe in the projects. I told her as much once or twice and she caught a big old attitude with me. We almost came to blows for my voicing this. The saying goes, 'A hit dog will holler'. Well Sha-Sha was hollering at the top of her lungs. I reminded myself I had my own problems and if she wanted to play the fool then so be it. I came to the conclusion to keep my mouth shut and my thoughts to myself. Whenever she complained about the child support or lack of it being gone, I would roll my eyes and change the subject. Let her find someone else to sing that sob story to. Until she demanded, bribed or used the court to petition more support for baby Yannique then I had no words for her.

The day we beat down Shatease mother was a Sunday. It started off as any other day. My newly found step-father, Robert, was cooking breakfast. The bacon was sizzling in the big black skillet. My younger siblings were arguing over who was going to play the winner on the PlayStation 3. My older brother Junior was Bo guarding the remote control as if to say, "None of you little ninjas taking this from me."

Groggily, I bumped and banged my way into the pale green bathroom with the yellow dotted shower curtains. Splashing cold water on my face, I stared in the mirror. I noticed bags were forming under my eyes. I made a mental note to stop drinking forty ounces of Old English with the guys. The saying, "Black don't crack" obviously didn't apply to drinkers. Take for instance, Ms. Boop from down the hall. She was twenty nine years old and had crow's feet and wrinkles already. A lot of the younger generation thought she was a witch. Sometimes they would knock her door and run. When I caught my siblings doing this I would swat them on the tail and hold my hand up as if to say, "I'm sorry."

After performing my morning bathroom ritual, I went in the kitchen and took some verbal jabs at Robert, "Hey old guy, you wash your hands? What you in here burning up this early in the morning?"

"You aren't saying anything but a word. You know dis ninja clean and cook well, burning anything, hardly! I am Chef Black r Dee in this piece," he countered while laughing. Robert had an old southern drawl about him. There were times it was hard to understand him. Today though was not one of them.

Robert then proceeded to the fridge, grabbed the dozen of eggs, a couple of slices of cheese then closed the door with his foot. Without missing a step, he grabbed a bowl from the dish drain, cracked five out of the dozen eggs and then began to whip them with a fork. We jokingly made small talk as I grabbed the orange juice from out the fridge and upturned it to my mouth. Just then baby Yannie, short for Yannique, ran in my apartment. Her pamper was hanging halfway off exposing a little pale butt cheek. Her hair was sticking on top of her head. Half was braided and half was a loose. A crack stem was in her little hand. I lost all resolve and stated, "I will fuckin' kill her."

Flying down the hallway after screaming for Shatease, who wound up spending the night with me after a late night of hanging in the lobbies, to follow me. She took one look at baby Yannie and got in high gear. With orange juice trailing down my chin, I bust into

Shatease and her mother's apartment. I saw her
mother coming towards the door yelling at Shatease
and me. I hooked off on her. She reeled back and it
was on. It was blow for blow at first until all the years
of embarrassment and frustration of her and my
mother's addictive antics surfaced. I wailed on her
with all my might. She started screaming for help.
Somehow, she got loose from my head lock and as I
rushed forward to snatch her ass back I slipped and
fell on what was once a puddle of spilled Kool- Aid.
She must have heard the thud because she stopped
short, turned and started moving in for the kill. It was
at this point Shatease became unglued from her spot
and kneed her mother in the midsection. She doubled
over and we both went in for the kill. Needless to say
she was a hot bloodied mess by the time Robert came
to break it up.

My mother comes gliding down the hall a couple of
minutes later like she was a saint, "Now, Bianca you
know children get into everything. I told you a
million times to clean this pig sty up. You trying to
make this child one of your crack babies, huh?"

Then my mother started rummaging through papers
left on the glass wall unit, "Maybe you can get your
boo, Guy, to clean this shit up. This house not fit for
children at all."

My mother, Angela, gave Bianca an evil ass look and
then went back to our apartment. I thought to myself

she is a fine one to talk. If it wasn't for me and my siblings with the help of Robert her place would be a wreck. All she did was lay in bed when she wasn't on a crack binge. Her room was a fucking mess. I seemed to be the only one who had the stomach to clean things up. I would be so frustrated and yell at the others in order to get them to help me.

I only wished I could clean up my mother's life the way I was able to clean up the apartment. Desperately missing the good old days when my mother was dressed to the nines, hair so fly and make up on point even the young boys tried to holler almost lost my composure. I started crying. I was crying because I know my mother was missing my father. I was missing him even more.

I understand grief. Leeq was a big part of my life as well. She may have lost a husband but I lost a father. It doesn't get any more lost than that. I was desperately hurting. It was as if I lost both parents. Because of my mother's crack habit she could hardly be deemed as a parent. I held the household down. Now that Robert was there he was a help to the running of the household as well.

Turning back around to deal with the matter at hand, I flinched at Bianca, "Clean this dirt trap the fuck up."

I grabbed Shatease and we left Bianca broken, beaten and hollering.

Empress Simone
IN THESE STREETS: KOI'S SAGA

Chapter 2

Shatease winded up staying at my apartment for about
a week. Due to the cramped up quarters and lack of
space, she and baby Yannie moved back in, down the
hall, with Bianca. However for the whole week they
were with us, Angela, my mother, showed her ass.
She went around like she was queen all day, barking
orders at me and my siblings and supervising Robert
in the kitchen while he was cooking. Telling him he
was making the bacon too crispy and the biscuits
should be put in the oven last because she didn't want
them cold as much as she didn't want them burnt.

She then took her hand and rubbed it across the top of
the wooden dish cabinets as if she were giving them
the white glove test, looked at her fingers and started
to talk in a loud, harsh tone, "This motherfucking
place need to be clean from top to bottom. I am so
disgusted. I stay on everyone to help me but still
come up with dirt."

She would then move to the one little four paned
window and move the yellowing cream curtains to the
side. She would crane her neck to peek out the

window and then bring it back real fast, "Humph, humph, humph, we need to do some redecorating around here so this place don't look like Bianca's pig sty she call a home."

My mother would then switch very fast and roughly going towards her room while yelling, "You damn kids pick these toys up and stay off of that video game for an hour or so."

Shatease and I would giggle at my mother's theatrics. I almost fainted when she made a half ass attempt to clean her room. I nudged Shatease, "You need to move in here more often. Seem you brought the cleaning bug and it bit her," I said and rolled my eyes.

"I wish Ms. Angela would stop playing. She is really doing too much and starting to scare me with this domestic shit she is on," Shatease stated.

We both started laughing and Sha-Sha, as I sometimes called her, went back to doing my hair. She was hooking me up with a twenty-four inch layered weave. I told her to put platinum blonde tracks in it. We were going to a house party this particular evening. I wanted to be the center of attraction. Shatease and I boosted our outfits for this occasion.

 Sha-Sha got a white haltered top jumpsuit that resembled a genie outfit at the bottom with a blue belt sewn on. The belt had stars and silver sparkles. She was going to accessorize with some blue pumps and wear her reddish hair in a side swept style. My choice of outfit was a little more revealing. It was a green v-top that showcased my firm breast with denim pum pum shorts that showed my pretty legs. I was going to keep the accessories simple with a thin necklace and tear drop earrings I bought from the pawn shop on 149th and Third Avenue in the Bronx and green espadrille wedged shoes on my feet.

I was into reggae music heavy now and was hoping the deejay would play some tunes tonight I could twerk my ass to. Everyone I knew was under the impression twerking is an American thing but in all actuality my mother told me how all dances originated from Africa. She said the Caribbean, specifically the island of Jamaica, then made dances such as wining and the tic famous. In reality these dances were an earlier form of twerking. I couldn't help but think to myself it was in my blood to show a bitch up on the dance floor. My mother's father was from St. Thomas, United States Virgin Islands, Charlotte Amalie to be exact. The food and music were embedded in my soul. If I smelled the food, I had to eat it; if I heard the music, I had to stop and wine my waist up in a gyrating motion no matter where I was. My new shit was Soca and Calypso…cent, five cent, ten cent, dollar. I loved that old time song. One thing my mother was good for is her taste in music. Yet, sometimes, I couldn't be bothered with her. There was something in my mind that no matter how peaceful the day was going, how much she remained sober, would flash back to the life we were living after my beloved King, Shaleeq MacDougal, my father passed. I would envision the men she would sometimes sneak out of her room thinking all us children were asleep. I would also envision her sucking dick the few times I would peek through the crack in her door when her company was visiting. I didn't understand how she could bring so many men around her children. These were neighborhood men from the projects. Some were married and some were outright junkies. The one thing they all had in common was the love of the drug crack and the need to pay for her ranking pussy. Yes, I was mad at my mother so sometimes she would laugh at me if I stopped dancing when she walked in a room, "I already saw you. Did you forget I am west-Indian myself? Your grandfather, my father, was a west-Indian man."

I usually wound up rolling my eyes and turning the radio off. I hated when she interrupted my 'moments'. Listening to my music was a form of therapy for me and as usual Ms. Angela Bettenfield ruined another thing in my life. My mother never noticed me rolling my eyes and would just keep on talking. Hurriedly, I would change the subject or leave the room saying, "I'll be back," but I would never return. She would yell down the hallway to my room five minutes later, "Little bit hurry up. I want us to dance together."

I would act like I didn't hear her. If she were really in the mood to spend some quality mother-daughter time she would knock on my room door. I would jump in my bed and feign sleep. My mother would simply push open the door, peek in, sigh and whisper, "Maybe next time."

This night of the party I had an eerie feeling. I informed Shatease of my feelings to which she simply stated, "Girl, stop worrying. Nothing is going to happen. We will be on our home court. Now hurry, let's get ready."

Shaking it off, I continued getting ready by showering then doing my makeup. Coming to the conclusion I wanted all eyes on me, chose a green eye shadow to go with my top. I went against wearing lip gloss and went gothic with Black lipstick. Shatease did her makeup earthy as usual. I told her we need to make a statement. We can't be looking all homely. She laughed at me and said making statements is what got her a baby at the age of thirteen.

"Listen bitch, Yannie is here now. Why you keep saying that like it's a bad thing? Her little high yellow ass is a blessing and you gone learn to let the circumstances go or I am going to tear you up."

"Hold up. Wait one damn minute, I don't know who you are talking to but she is my baby. I am speaking on the circumstance that brought her about and not her as an actual living person. You need to see things more than just one way; which is your way when there is a world of other people who might be right. Educated people who know what they are speaking about," Shatease said. She then huffed and started slamming flat irons and hair spray bottles on the wooden chest with missing knobs. The thirteen inch TV started to shake. I told her to calm her ass down. She stopped, looked at me and threw her hands on her hips, "Yea, whatever," was all she said.

I saw when she rolled her eyes up in her head. Shatease started mumbling under her breath. I came to the conclusion it might be better to let my rider have her moment then get in her ass and ruin both our nights.

We let a whole thirty minutes of not talking to each other and slamming things pass by before she broke the silence, "Listen Koi, to some extent I understand what you are saying. I did not nor do I intend any harm when saying those things. I love my child or I wouldn't have had her. You have to learn to be easy. Of course I have some resentment towards the way she was brought into the world. I have resentment towards the way her father denies her. However, that was the circumstance and not the child. I love her. You get it Koi? I love baby Yannie. I wouldn't trade

[27]

her for anything in the world. Not even for your stinking ass. You feel me?"

We shoulder bumped each other, "Yes, I feel you sexy. Now let's get ready. We have some bitches who waiting to hate on us and dudes ready to spend on us. Ya heard me?" I said to Sha-Sha assuring her there weren't any harsh feelings for the words exchanged between us.

Once ready, we made the call to Kemo, the weed dealer. We got three dime sacks. I broke down the weed while she split the white owls. Then I rolled the weed up nice and tight in the cigars. I stashed three blunts for when I came home and needed a boost to my highness. Tonight I wouldn't be able to pop a Percocet unless I snuck one. Shatease didn't believe in any harsh drugs. I respected that about her but also knew it had something to do with the circumstances surrounding her pregnancy with baby Yannie. I was the type who would try anything once except crack. I guess I was scared of crack seeing the way it had our parents.

The party was in Mott-Haven, a neighboring project. Shatease didn't seem to be worried about a damn thing but I was. We had a little mini beef with some local girls by the name of Sapphire and Kiki. I had to lay the smack down on Sapphire over some work she messed up for Griff. Kiki and Shatease winded up jumping in. It was an all-out battle between the sets of best friends. It was so intense that Kiki pulled out a knife on us,

"You want me to cut your pretty faces?" she asked Shatease and me. We shook our heads no as this was the first time this ever happened to us. I saw an evil grin slide in on her face. Feeling a little punked, I came to the conclusion I would die with honor and not like a sucker. Reaching out to grab the knife, she raised it over her head and that is when my foot instinctively went up and caught her in the midsection. She doubled over. Shatease and I pounced on her for dear life. We never even saw when Sapphire smashed a bottle and started swinging it wildly like a mad woman.

"Get the fuck off her before I start poking you young hoes."

Thinking my rider and I already proved our point, tapped Sha-Sha and said, "Come on," then turning to Sapphire emphasized, "This shit isn't over. You going to regret pulling shit out on me. Like this bitch here just did."

We walked the short distance back to my apartment. There we vowed to never let another bitch get the drop on us again. We put in a call to Mack, my uncle; my father's half-brother. I explained the situation thoroughly, "Yea," he agreed, "This could get very ugly niece. I will see you within the week to bring you some protection."

Mack, true to his word showed up with a new, shiny glock 9mm and full clip. He showed me the workings of the nine. I never felt more elated than when I see that shiny life snatcher.

Mack also had a lock box he told me to keep it in. He stressed the importance of keeping it from my younger siblings and older handicapped brother. My uncle also told me he lost his heart when he lost his brother Leeq and he didn't want to lose another member of his family. I reassured him he shouldn't worry. I had it all under control. I placed the nine in the lock box and put it in the top of my closet towards the back. I placed some of my clothing in front of it in an attempt to conceal it. My uncle Mack and I talked for a while longer then he gave me four hundred dollars and left.

Snapping out of my reverie, as Sha-Sha and I walked past the benches in front of the building I noticed a group of onlookers. Some were rolling their eyes; some were whispering. Upon closer inspection, I noticed it was Kiki of all people. I rolled my eyes at her and continued to the building.

Shatease and I got on the elevator and pressed for the fifth floor, "Can you believe that hoe? She all pointing and whispering. I know that bitch ass is soft as fuck for not setting it off. She must have remembered that pouncing we gave her on her own home court."

"Huh, what are you talking about Koi?" Shatease stated making me upset, "Bitch, did you not just see Kiki out front with them hags?" I said rolling my eyes and snaking my neck.

"I am hardly stunting that bitch. She don't really want it or she would have set it off like you said. Come on Koi. Get it together. I want to enjoy my night without thinking of some scaly wags."

"Okay, bae you got it," I told her coming to the conclusion I worried too much. I also figured it wasn't anything but a hop, skip and a jump to get to my building and snatch the nine mill if females seemed to get out of hand, "I really hope we see some new ballers tonight. The thugs on the block are getting played out."

"I know you didn't just say played out? Really Koi, you got the one with the most clout and paper. What are you really complaining for?" Shatease asked me in disbelief.

"He may have the most clout but he also have the most pussy being thrown at him. I am frustrated. I have to put on airs in front of people, especially in front of Nakisha. I am glad I wound up tagging her ass. However, that's his wifey, so I have to be understanding and don't pass my place. Plus with our age difference I don't want him in any trouble. I am just feeling all type of ways about our time together. So until I get to be in that number one spot I am just

[31]

going to pout a little, flirt with other dudes a little and wait it out. No harm, no foul, I am not fucking these other dudes or anything. I am just letting them spend a little paper on me. Well us, because you know I don't go anywhere without you. You are my road dog."

Shatease just shook her head and then the elevator doors opened. It seemed the house party was in full effect. There were people in the hallways smoking blunts; some even had red cups in their hands. The Dee jay was blasting Drake's song, 'Zero to a Hundred'.

Shatease and I got on the end of the line to gain admittance inside the apartment. We faced each other and made small talk as we brushed one another's hair, trying to ensure our styles were up to grade A inspection. We also checked each other's teeth and made sure there were no traces of lipstick on them. We patted each other on our thigh-hip area and said to one another, "Looking gorgeous rider."

We started to giggle as we zoomed in on the other hood rat's attire. Some girls' outfits were on point and others made us wonder how their friends allowed them out the house wearing such clothes.

We took special note and consideration of teasing one red bone girl. Her hair was in a basic wrap style. It seemed she tried to emulate the look of the great late singer Aaliyah. She sported a pair of black spandex leggings with a beige top. It was hard to decipher if the top was a halter or tie up. It seemed to be both. What really made Shatease and I crack up laughing is she had jellies on her feet. We know they were trying to bring that type of shoe back in style. However, they looked to be something my mother would wear. They were a thick plastic like material with an egg shell white color and had a silver buckle on the side,

"Now you know that don't make any damn sense," Shatease said laughing and pointing. Some other people on the line caught on and started laughing as well.

"Word, right, home girl need to go back to 1979 with all that," a big burly but sexy ass chocolate female said. The two friends with her all joined in with us as we high fived each other and laughed amongst a circle.

Somehow the object of our ridicule must have caught on because she started shaking her leg really fast and putting one foot on top of the other. I took this action to be her way of trying to hide her shoes. She started shaking her head along with her leg. Another girl and dude about Griff's age started to glare at us. The dude looked familiar but I couldn't figure out where I knew him from. My eyes fell on the multi colored beads around his neck. I thought, 'aw shit he's affiliated.'

Yet, in true Koi fashion, I became louder, "I want to know who these ninjas looking at?"

The dude shook his head, sucked his teeth but turned back around after the other female whispered something in his ear.

"Oh, Just like I figured. I knew they didn't want it," I said even bolder.

Someone must have informed the host Janice I was in the hallway about to get in someone's ass because she came flying out the apartment and straight over to me, Shatease and my newfound crew.

"Koi, ma, what's good? I didn't know you were out here until I heard you was starting something. Please come on in and let all that slide. It's my twenty fourth birthday and I want to enjoy myself. I have some Patron by the Dee jay booth. Follow me and I will give you and your peeps a shot on the house. You know I am charging two dollars for every drop," she said and started laughing.

I told Shatease and my newfound crew to come on and follow Janice and me. We went to the Dee jay area and she lined us up two shots each. We threw them back so fast and looked at her, I am sure her head started spinning.

Janice shook her head, "Okay, one more round and you all have to pay for the next go round," she said while tipping the bottle to each shot glass.

"Good looking," Shatease told her. We then threw the hot clear liquid down our throats.

"Catch you later," I told Janice while grabbing Shatease by the hand and leading her to the middle of the living room which was currently a make shift dance floor. The red living room furniture was out of the apartment except for one love seat. Janice had it blocking the area going towards the bedrooms but clear of the bathroom doorway. She had streamers in a variety of colors, which reminded me of the gay pride flag, running from all corners of the ceiling to meet in the middle as a drop. She had a miniature disco ball with the same colors spinning. The living room was also illuminated red by the light bulbs she had in the sockets. I almost gagged when I saw the birthday banners on the wall. I thought she said twenty four not twelve. Oh well to each their own. To me some adults just couldn't face the fact of getting older. They tried with all their might to hold on to their youth.

As Shatease and I danced with our newfound crew, the odor of body sweat and variety of cheap perfumes hit my nostrils. I scrunched up my nose and told the crew let's take our little huddle next to the free space near an open window. They happily agreed. We danced to the song 'I'm in love with the coco'. Suddenly, mid-way through the song, the middle of the living room illuminated from the front door opening. When I looked up toward the direction the light was coming from I gasped from the shock of seeing Griff whispering sweet nothings in Kiki's ear.

My feelings were confirmed when he wiggled his tongue near her ear. As I stared at his actions I noticed his hand which had been above on her waist suddenly dipped lower. His hand was now cupping her ass. She threw her head back and touched him ever so gently on the shoulder as if to say, "You are too much or oh, you are so funny."

I was devastated. Instead of trying to play it off I told Shatease to look at the two idiots over by the door. She shook her head in disbelief while saying, "I don't believe this shit. She just trying to get some payback for that ass kicking. Kiki know beyond a doubt Griff's your dude." \

"I am so hurt, right now," I said standing close to her and whispering in her ear loudly so she could hear me over the deejay music, "I want to go home and just climb in the bed right now."

"Oh no you don't bitch," she reached in her strapless bra and pulled out a fresh blunt. She pulled her lighter out as well. Then proceeded to spark it up when she was interrupted.

"Damn, ma what else you have in there?" the burly sexy chocolate laughingly asked her. We soon found out her name was Monae. She lived in Far Rockaway, Queens but was chilling with her cousins tonight. I giggled even though I wasn't in a good mood. This was because Shatease was notorious for never carrying a purse but stuffing her bra with all her items.

I just always felt she had enough titties and didn't need anything else in there.

"Glad to see you are better," Shatease told me, "Never let a dude who let it be known you can't be anything more than a homie or a side of ass, see you sweat, especially if he is with a next bitch. You shake, shake, shake that ass girl and give him something to sweat," she said while dancing and sticking her ass out. Then looking back and slapping at it.

The more I thought on things the more correct she seemed to be. My problem laid in the fact Griff was rubbing up and whispering in my enemy's ear. For those reasons I was upset. Griff was perfectly aware of Kiki and my history. Not too many people from the hood didn't know of the brawl. Some felt Shatease and I were wrong for jumping on her but a lot felt she was wrong for pulling out the knife in the first place. That is just how the hood gets down anyway. Everyone have an opinion about your life but don't have the heart or the soul to endure all the things you endure.

I mean my father, my king was shot and killed right in front of my eyes and I am supposed to sweat or worry about doing a next bitch dirty? Did the killer who shot my father care about my family when I was younger? Did the killer wonder who was going to feed my father's children and unborn child, his pregnant wife, or show his handicapped son some sense of manhood on any level he might be able to attain? So why, I wondered did anyone think I should even care about a beating I put on a punk ass bitch with a knife?

Shaking my anger and millions of questions off, I decided to get into the groove by taking Sha-Sha's advice. I maneuvered my way through the crowd toward this dude named Fuquan. He was a Black Indian cutie, I heard my Jamaican friends call him a coolie. He was born of Jamaican parents' right here in the United States of America but still claimed he was Jamaican. Fuquan only talked with an accent when he spoke to his parents or elders in his family.

Fuquan's features helped me reach this decision to rendezvous with him tonight. His skin was smooth and light, his hair was neatly braided. When he wore his hair loose on certain days it was wavy and mad long. His eyes were dark and so were his lips. I think his lips were that color from all the weed he smoked. He was a chain smoker for real. Fuquan had me beat to a punch. He was a rugged pretty boy. The type people in the hood dared not mess with. Much like my family, if he lost a fight there were fifty motherfuckers coming for your jaw.

He was dressed in black cargo pants, with big pockets on the side, a pair of fresh black Jordan's and a crisp white wife beater. He had on one medium sized chain with a Jesus head piece, two diamond stud earrings in his left ear and one pinky ring.

Fuquan was the type to stay on fleek; once or twice a couple of neighborhood thugs, who wasn't cool with him, tried to rob him or set him up. He handled his own in one robbery attempt but got stomped out in the other. When he confirmed who set him up for that robbery, let's just say they were in the hospital for a minute.

Snapping out of my reverie on his hood antics, I placed my hand by his ear and started to whisper, "hey daddy, you happy to see your girl?" I asked the seventeen year old Fuquan all the while rubbing his dick. He swatted my hand away leaving me temporary flustered. He shook his head and bent down whispering back in my ear, "Yo, chill Koi. My baby momma is up in here. I will get with you later."

Totally upset I rolled my eyes and told him don't bother. By this time as I checked the spot Kiki and Griff were last in, I took note on how he now had her pinned to the wall with one hand tickling her breast and the other plastered on the wall up above their heads. She was laughing then our eyes connected. The bitch had the nerve to wink her eye at me. Then she turned her attention back to Griff and started to tease his mouth with her tongue. She whispered something and pointed in my direction. He turned to look and then the ninja just shrugged his shoulders. I couldn't help it and the tear dam over flowed. I ran back to the huddle and told Shatease what happened. She wiped my eyes, and then pointed at Fuquan who was walking in our direction.

He grabbed me around my waist, "I sent her home Muffin," he whispered directly in my ear so I could hear him over the music playing.

"Great, light us up," I said hugging him back. We hugged up all night dancing to the fast songs and gyrating to the slow songs. The sorry ass deejay only played two reggae songs so our bump n grind session ended faster than it started. We slobbed each other down as Shatease and our new found crew danced with each other and various teen boys who possessed the heart to approach them. All in all, it was a good night for us. As I made the attempt to secretly rendezvous with Fuquan at his mother's apartment Shatease grabbed my arm,

"Yo, Griff just called, He was pissed! He said it's imperative we meet him in our building lobby."

"Nah, not now whatever is going on could wait. I am going home with Fuquan. It's four in the morning isn't nothing wrong except Kiki fronting on the ass and Nakisha is on her period so he horny," I stated disturbed at the fact he could shrug his shoulders in an apparent disregard for my feelings. Why should I be at his beck in call?

"I am telling you right now is not the time to hold grudges. He stated William and the Rough Houser's ran up on Beemie in the building exit. They laid three shots to him and bodied him with a head shot. He's hurting right now. Said he need his riders to set some dudes up from Patterson Projects in retaliation. I don't think he is straight or horny right now," she informed me.

"Damn, not Beemie. That's his baby brother. Damn," I said undecided as to if I wanted to forgive him and put Fuquan on the back burner. I was in love with my blood dude, Griff. I didn't have to think too long. I went back to Fuquan and told him business was calling. He smiled and assured me he understood. Being the hood dude he was I didn't expect him not to. We slobbed each other down for a moment until Shatease interrupted again by telling me to come on. He patted me hard on my ass and told me he would catch me later.

Chapter 3

Shatease was beyond upset. I knew she had slight feelings for Beemie and judging by her reaction it seemed as if they ran deep. She was going on and on during the short distance to our building stating things like if the Rough Houser's were bold enough to come to our building then it was time for us to put that work in. We suffered a loss of life on our side that we shouldn't let go without retaliating. That hit a button with me and being the rider I was, I couldn't let my dude go without a soldier. If he needed me to set someone up he just needed to consider it done. I bet Kiki didn't have the heart or balls to do half the shit Griff needed done; just knowing that I had something over his other bitches, especially Nakisha made me giddy.

I was his rider, his female soldier, his youngest in command! Needless to say, I would kill a person if need be!

When Shatease and I made it to the building, by the look of things Griff wasn't holding up too well. He was swinging his hands and punching the walls. There were obvious dents in the mail boxes. His eyes were a bloody red and his knuckles were blood soaked as well. There were stains on his shirt as well as scratches on his face. He looked like he was in a rumble.

I knew he was at the party with Kiki. Between that time and now was only two hours. I figured that Beemie got shot earlier in the evening for him to know the exact specifics of the shooting. Then again he was shot in the projects and news by word of mouth travelled quickly. Shatease and I were hurt having to see Griff in so much pain. He noticed us, shook his head rapidly then grabbed the side of his head with both hands. He dropped to the floor sobbing. It was a dry sob that seemed endless. My heart was pounding. Try as I might, couldn't find the right words to say to ease his pain. I honestly could relate to him. I did the one thing I wanted someone to do when I lost my King Shaleeq, I ran over to him and threw my arms around his neck. I held on to him for dear life as he was sitting on the lobby floor. He wrapped his strong arms around the bottom of my legs and held on just as tightly.

Passerby's stared as they walked. They whispered among themselves wondering what happened. A few had the audacity to stop and actually ask what was going on. His friend Mike unable to take anymore simply told them, "Keep it moving homie. There is nothing to see here!!"

Some left peacefully but others were bolder saying things like 'You don't own this lobby.'

Mike being unable to take anymore grabbed one dude up and banged him hard into the lobby elevator. He went to hit him but Shatease stopped him, "No Mike stop. We don't need you in jail. Griff is going to need you. Think about it."

Mike let the man go. He smoothed the man's clothing and then patted him extra hard in his chest, "sorry my brother, nothing to see here."

He then abruptly grabbed him by the shoulder turned him around and kicked him square in the ass, "Get to fucking stepping now player."

We were finally able to get Griff up off the floor. We took him to Mike house since there were less people there. He lived in a quaint one bedroom with his grandmother Marie. She converted the living room into a room for him by placing a twin bed in a corner. They did have a futon and a small 19' TV with one cable box. The TV and cable box sat on a Black end coffee table. The tiles in the apartment was also black. They did have red curtain panels in the windows. They were the old antique looking type that had a gold string. I figured to tie the curtains back. It reminded me of a belted rope. He kept the whole apartment immaculate since she was unable to move

with agility due to age. Marie would walk around the
house at times, fanning herself and saying, "Thank
the Lord for this child. Thank Jesus, yes thank him."

Mike would smile. He lost his mother at a young age.
She was hit by a drunk driver while crossing the street.
As a result he went to live with his grandmother
Marie. He doted on his grandmother. She was strict
when he was younger and even though he acted out to
the neighborhood children, he straightened up when
he saw Marie. He was brutal to others to the point
sometimes it was funny. If a fellow playmate's parent
told Marie that Mike was acting up he was merciless
on the child with the punches, "Tell your
motherfucking mother to mind her business. Next
time it's going to be worse. Do you understand me?"

The kid would usually cry and shake his head running
away. True to form if the parent snitched again and it
resulted in a spanking for Mike, he would usually
strip the child of some article of clothing and throw it
down an incinerator. Shatease and I rarely worried
about our mothers snitching on anyone. They were
too busy chasing the dragon called 'Crack' to worry
about Mike and his bullish ways.

Secretly, Shatease and I admired their relationship.
Marie would come in the living room during certain
days and would spend quality time with Mike
watching 'The Price is Right' or 'Who wants to be a
Millionaire'. Whichever show they watched was

contingent upon her mood that day. She stopped watching the afternoon soap-operas long ago because she felt like her life started to revolve around them. Mike's grandmother Marie would even schedule her doctor's appointments around the time her show came on. This would ensure she never missed an episode. Marie would even converse with her longtime neighbor and confidante. Honestly, I feel she stopped watching the show once her confidante passed. It just wouldn't be the same. I know this from experience.

Once in Mike's apartment, we plopped Griff on the futon. Mike told us to keep the noise level down for a moment while he went to talk with his granny.

"It's late and although I understand he has faced a great loss you guys will keep the noise down, while I rest up. You give Griffin my condolences, you hear me boy?" Marie stated in a stern but loving way.

"Yes, big ma. I hear you and we understand. No noise above city regulations. I am just kidding. I love you and thank you."

Mike then came back in the living room laughing because his grandma threw a slipper at him for his snide remark. He loved her feistiness. Mike assessed his friend a little more closely,

"Yo, bro we need to get the soldiers ready. We can't let this ride. Once we take care of this you going to feel better. It's like when Kemo's brother Ray was killed in East New York. No one ate or slept until we bodied those niggas," he said trying to get Griff's mind on revenge mode.

"Word, Mike. Exactly what I am feeling right now. Someone have to pay," Griff said and turned to me to continue, "Koi, little mama, this is how you can help me. I need for you to get some heavy artillery from your Uncle Mack. Tell him you need it. Fuck, tell him it's a matter of life or death. See if he can give you warehouse prices. A nigga little hard up for cash being I just re upped on my product. I would hate to have to pull a robbery, get caught and can't ride for Beemie. Word to Blood they going to hate they violated mine," he punched his right hand into his left and made a grunting sound.

I told him I believe I can get my Uncle Mack to help us on this mission by supplying the armor. However, I wasn't too sure if he would come down on the prices because he was about his money. If not mistaken he overcharged people. I heard my mother numerous times with him asking him to do her a favor and lower the prices for one friend or another. My uncle never did accommodate her. Mike shook his head vigorously side to side. Saying he didn't want to hear that.

Griff needed me to come through for him no matter what it took to do it. To make Griff feel better I told him that I would try my best. I rubbed his head and put my forehead to his and started to gently kiss him while intensely staring in his eyes. I pulled his arm around me and snuggled into his chest. I pulled my legs up on the futon and rubbed his manhood. Although he was upset, he allowed me to show him this form of intimacy. I was ready and eager to orally please him if need be. I would do this even in front of Shatease and Mike. I didn't hold any punches when it came to Griff and he knew this. However, he was content with me sitting under his arm caressing him.

He animatedly talked with Mike. They were discussing what soldiers would be down to murder a rival Rough Houser. I took note of the names. There was Donnie, Milk and Bam. Donnie was the O.G. of the squad but Bam and Milk were wild and crazy. I called them the wild cards. I sort of perked up and became antsy when Mike said they might need Fuquan to be in charge of the young ones. Hoping secretly Griff didn't see Fuquan and me embracing. I became tense when I felt his eyeballs on me so I looked up and asked him why he had that look on his face?

"Yo, don't play with me," Griff stated, "I saw you hugged up with Fu earlier. What was that all about? Don't think because I lost my brother I won't get in your ass. You still better stay in your lane or deal with the consequences."

Instantly I became defensive. I wanted to get in his ass about Kiki yet I didn't want him to unleash his fury on me. Griff sometimes was a beast when he was mad. His licks were worse than my cousins. As a result, I simply stated, "You are a fine one to talk, seeing as though that hoe Kiki had your undivided attention. Before you lie, I think we need to end this conversation." Griff agreed by turning his attention back to Mike. He reiterated all the reasons to call Fuquan for this mission. The main reason being Fuquan was wild and crazy. At seventeen years old, Griff and Mike, felt he had the heart of a lion to keep even the O.G. Donnie in check.

Donnie was known to sip on Lean, which was made by mixing cough syrup, jolly Ranchers candy and soda. Most people call it Sizzurp, because of his Sizzurp intake he needed constant nudges to combat the drowsiness it caused. Due to a seizure he suffered once from his consumption of Sizzurp his reaction time was slower than before he met his fate.

Despite these things he was ruthless in his torture methods. He once shot a man's balls off for smacking his little sister's ass. In short, everyone in Mitchell knew he was certifiably crazy or seven thirty as was the slang term. His younger sisters had free reign to mess or bully who they chose because no one wanted to go against Donnie. Well, almost no one and he was from Mott Haven not Mitchell Projects and that was my homey, lover, friend Fuquan.

Griff and Mike talked over what type of retaliation they wanted to deal out on William and the Rough Houser's. The pair came to the conclusion they wanted to do a Cali type drive by.

For this type of retaliation, Griff stressed to me that Mack needed to be able to get Military style firearms. Off the top of his head he wanted a Singapore originated automatic weapon. This was a submachine type gun. It required a thirty round detachable box magazine and fired at least nine hundred rounds per minute. It was also a type of compact personal weapon. He said after the job was finished Shatease and my job would be to dispose of the weapons. Griff stressed the importance of not stuffing it down the manhole or sewer drain. We had seen enough sweeps of the area after a gun battle to know the cops will look down there.

Being in love with the description of the gun felt it wouldn't hurt if I stashed it out the house. I felt I might need to put my gun game on Kiki's hating ass. I was going to be just the gun clapper to do it.

Griff cried on and off for the rest of our time at Mike's apartment. During his storm we all told our memories of Beemie. We remembered his smile, his laughter, his knuckle game and most importantly we remembered him as our brother. Griff and Mike finalized the plan and made decisions as to who in the crew would be used for pinpointing their whereabouts, luring them all into one secluded spot, who would drive and who the trigger man would be. It was decided Donnie was the expendable one and should do the shooting. Fuquan was the trusted one and would lure them all to the spot under the pretense of a dice game. Griff was just going to chill in the back seat making sure the shooter hit the marks. We left after realizing it was twelve in the afternoon. Mike's grandmother came out her room, kissed Griff and hugged him then told Mike he had to help her to the supermarket. She wanted to cook for Griff's family during their time of bereavement. My hungry ass looked at her when she addressed me, "Ma'am do you mind if me and my cousin come back for some of your food."

Griff face registered total shock, Mike chuckled and Shatease pushed me in the back of my head.

"Aren't you Angela's baby girl?" she asked me squinting her eyes trying to get a better look.

"Yes, ma'am I am," I hesitantly stated. I really didn't know if my mother tried to harm her or anything while chasing her demons.

Marie looked at me then sighed heavily, "Sure sweetie, you and your cousin can come back around seven. I will make enough to send a little on over to your little brother and sister. You know I used to babysit your father when he was a little boy. It broke my heart how your mother is carrying on after his death. I pray for her and you often. I am glad to talk to you. Always know you have someone praying for you.

Now you all run along and let Griff get some proper rest and Mike is going to accompany me to the grocery store. I swear these ham hocks not going to jump from the store into my pot on their own. Also Griff, we all was raised on pork so I don't want to hear none of that mess these young new age Black folk talking about, no pig and crap." Marie rolled her eyes and placed her hands on her hips laughing.

We all had no choice but to laugh with her. Standing up I grabbed Shatease by the arm and dragged her to the area Marie was standing at. I threw my free arm around her shoulder and kissed her on the cheek saying, "Ma'am, I thank you for letting us come back. Most importantly I thank you for praying for my family. With that being said, my cousin and I are going to get out your hair."

I waved by to the guys then Shatease and I high tailed it out the door and made it to my apartment in record time. Exhausted we ran into my room and kicked my little brother and sister out making them take baby Yannie with them.

Chapter 4

If I wasn't in such puppy love, I could have seen he would never leave Nakisha to be with me. Griff's motto, in which he stated more than once was, everyone served a purpose in someone's life. Everyone's purpose also had a different priority.

To Griff, I was just a mere soldier with benefits. In his dealings with me he received the benefit of hook-ups with my Uncle Mack, a well-respected gun smuggler. Griff also received the pleasure of any sexual intimacy offered him while eating his cake with other women. I fussed sometimes then other times I let who he was fucking ride. I was young but saw enough relationships die from a woman's nagging. I vowed to never be that way with the man I cared about.

I was a child playing a grown woman's game. Nakisha was significantly older than I and also him. She was twenty two years old, employed and went to college part time. She was any young dope boy's dream although she had a bit of a temper. Griff told me on an occasion Nakisha gave him re-up money when his workers came up short. In some cases the workers even had their daily pot taken by corrupt

[53]

Police Officers or Pigs as we called them. Each time or scenario, Nakisha covered the cost of the loss. He claimed her exact words were, 'I want to see my baby winning.'

Griff also told me he was in love with the way she was ghetto but classy. He coined the term 'Sophisticated Ratchet'. This simply meant she could speak proper English around corporate types or on job interviews but would curse a motherfucker out while snaking her neck and popping her gum in the hood.

My heart and soul were headed for turmoil. Matter of fact they were half-way there. I was only fourteen and a half but my hormones were raging. Griff didn't help matters much. He only fanned the flames on my desires to be with him. We would spend stolen moments in the project stairways, usually leading to the roofs or basements. There we would frolic without the act of penetration. We would dry hump so much his penis got a sore spot on it from rubbing the material in his jeans. He said sometimes boxers restricted him and he would like for his nut sac to sag and dick to swing freely. I would laugh at him. He was the type to talk really animated with every hand gesture possible to match the words which came out his mouth.

I remember the first time I sucked his dick. After a couple of awkward sucks and slurps he told me to spit on it, then told me to lick the sides of his shaft. After another couple of moments he put the tip of his dick back to my lips. My mouth immediately opened in response. He pushed it in a little roughly then commanded I suck it. I told him that is what I have been doing.

He mumbled, "Barely."

I rolled my eyes at him, smirked and commenced to sucking fervently again. It must have started feeling good to him because he interlocked his big brown hands behind my head then started pushing with enough force to make me suck even faster. He threw his head back, "Damn, baby. Ah yea, like that. Suck harder Koi. Harder," was all I heard.

Before I knew it, Griff screams out, "Yea, Yes," then hot, milky white fluid hit the back of my throat. I was shocked and a little disgusted. I looked up ready to flip out on him but gazing into his brown eyes, that sparkled, also noticing the glistening of his pearly white teeth in a mouth that was smiling widely helped me realize by doing this I made him happy. I took making Griff happy, seriously. Therefore I didn't dare complain but relished in the moment.

He mushed my forehead and then demanded, "Swallow it," For some reason, that rooftop encounter made me aim for status of 'Fire Head giver'. I could wait on the penetration. As long as I was giving him something those other chicks failed at; I knew I

secured my permanent place in Griff's heart. Fuck his
main chick Nakisha.

It was times like this I thought where did my
insatiable sexual appetite come from; the willingness
to play side chick? I often wondered, was it seeing
my mother with many different men before she
decided to be with Robert. Was being a slut
hereditary? Did it make me a slut if I was only
dealing with Griff?

I came to the conclusion to stop worrying about such
things. I was going to concentrate on making money,
my siblings and proving to Griff he didn't need any
female but me. Not only was I versatile but an asset to
him. My job was to make him see things my way. I
could flip a package, enforce his rule of come correct
or get slaughtered. Most importantly I could fulfill his
sexual needs. Right now, what else did a nineteen
year old boy need? The answer to that question I
would find out the hard way.

It was evident there would always be a difference in
the way Nakisha and I were treated. This was
confirmed whenever I saw them go out on occasion.
Griff showed Nakisha off around his friends and
family. All I received were stolen moments in
staircases and hallway exits; there were other times
that he would sneak me into his friend's apartment.
His friend's father was a part time security guard.
Sometimes he would get called to work to cover for

other workers. In these rare times he would rent the father's room. We would pop Percocet or smoke a blunt. Then it was my head game after that. Griff tried more than once to penetrate but it wouldn't go in. When I say he was packing, I mean he was packing.

In talking with my other friends who had already lost their virginity, it was admitted Griff was a monster and a beast in the bedroom. Having learned he beat up some of their pussies already, I was ready to go to war. However, after simmering I inquired as to if they were still fucking. Their answers were an insistent no. In the projects you ran the risk of this happening. Everyone knew each other but not everyone was loyal to each other. A lot of times, especially females broke the code of hands off the other's guy.

I came to the conclusion since Griff was no longer dealing with these chicks to let my anger go and move on. I told them that the past was the past. However, if I found out they were still fooling with my dude in any way I was laying hands on them. They knew of my wrath when angered. On more than one occasion these chicks witnessed me put the smack down on someone who tried to test me or my family. They even saw the bruise under Nakisha's eye. For a teen to black the eye of an adult they realized I was no joke when it came to fighting.

I huffed and puffed most of that day. Eventually, I got over hearing they slept with Griff and moved on.

My plans were simple and I realized something had to give. Gathering my feelings and trying my best to keep my hands to myself, I told my friends they had to get out. I got ready for the meeting with my Uncle and Griff. Today was the day the gun Griff so desperately wanted would exchange hands.

Griff was sort of upset with me. He felt I could get him a better deal on this submachine gun. I tried to relay to him this was a new, fresh out the box gun. Not only was it clean without any bodies it was a military type of weapon. Due to these reasons it was not cheap. It was a great risk to my Uncle even to be able to come up with this weapon. I felt he needed to be appreciative.

Griff still huffed and complained, "Naw, I'm not trying to hear that. The most I should be paying is five bills. This nigga got me paying twelve hundred. What type of fool he thinks I am?"

"Griff, listen I hear you bae. However, as my Uncle told me this is the type of gun those fool white guys be having. You know the ones who don't want the government to put restrictions on their guns. Now you know for us to be able to get our hands on them it's not going to be cheap," I said trying to reassure him that my family held him to the highest regard. In other words I was stroking his ego. If he wasn't in his feelings he would see I was correct. I understand he lost Beemie and was hurt. I just needed him to be fair.

Griff and I went back and forth for a little while. I moved in closer about to steal a kiss from his big juicy lips. Then I heard my Uncle's code knock and jumped back.

"Come in Uncle Mack," I said screaming. Once my Uncle was in the door I made the introductions. My uncle, gave Griff a dap.

"My niece speaks highly of you Mr. Gruff," my Uncle stated pronouncing Griff's name wrong.

"Unc, it's Griff not Gruff," I said clearing it up.

"Oh, does she?" Griff asked with a big cheese grin on his face, "I think highly of her as well. Did she tell you I do what I can to help the family?"

By the looks of my Uncle's face he didn't like what he was hearing. He cleared his throat and it went about ten octaves deeper, "Oh, you do now? Curious to know in what capacity? I lay bread on my sis in law Angela every two weeks. You mean to tell me they still need help?"

I tried to play it off. However, I was thinking that is why my mother was taking it easy. She got in good with Mack again and he has been hitting her off. If I knew this tidbit of information, I wouldn't be in the stores boosting so much or in the hallways holding drug dealer's packages. I was putting myself at risk when I could be home with my siblings. My mother was a trip. Not wanting to mess up my mother's little scheme further I tried to cover up her lies.

"Uncle Mack, now you know how it is. Food don't always last until the end of the month. No matter how much you buy, there will always be a day where the cupboards are bare. Plus, Junior eat so much you would think he was a grown man and not a boy. Then the younger ones need new shoes and clothes. I get my clothes and things however I can, which is usually boosting and things. Trust me momma need more than the average chick. She has four kids and just kicked a crack habit, Momma been clean for a while now."

I was crossing my fingers behind my back hoping not to get struck by lightning. I knew my mother just had a hit last night. She and Bianca was in here doing their crack dance, scratching their skin and looking all bugged eye. The two heifers were talking through clenched teeth. We all had a hard time trying to understand what the pair was trying to say.

"Hmm, hmm," my Uncle Mack said not fully believing me, "Now Gruff, I mean Griff, I thank you homeboy for helping my brother's family, my family. You just give me the bill and I will handle it. My brother Leeq was my heart. We being half -brothers doesn't matter; I am his keeper. That mean now that he is gone, I do my part and his part to see the family is alright. Due to certain situations I haven't been around. As with any family there will be fights but I'm back. So you feel free to hit me up. In light of all this I will go on and take four hundred off the price of this bad boy."

My uncle then took a box out of his satchel and opened it. The box held a shiny new compact submachine gun. I smiled to myself when I noticed Griff's expression. He was like a spoiled kid in a candy store.

"This will be the only time I mix business with pleasure. Just know from this day forward you are to pay the price I set. I am telling you now so that we won't have any discourse between us. Again I appreciate you looking out for my family but from here on out my family and our business are separate. Got it? If you agree to those terms there will be more beauties like this here in the box."

Griff was elated. I could tell by the sparkle in his eye and the smile across his face.

"Yes sir. I understand you and I hear you loud and clear. You have the magazine rounds as well?" he asked my uncle. My uncle confirmed and threw in an extra round for the heck of it I guess.

We conversed some once the initial business was concluded. Griff became misty eyed as he talked to my uncle about his brother Beemie's death. Griff stated he was still in some sort of state of shock or denial. He said sometimes when his cell phone ring he swears it's his baby brother. He stated he is always near the point of traumatization when it isn't.

My uncle told him he knew the pain all too well. That is how he felt about my King Leeq. He told him don't ever expect to get over the loss completely but as days go by things will get a tad bit easier. In the meantime, until that happens, expect to cry buckets of tears. Uncle Mack emphasized to Griff the importance of letting his grief out even in a public places.

He said real men had feelings and they should express them. My uncle also stated the anger will eat him up and corrode him if he didn't let the grief out. Griff explained Beemie's services weren't until Friday of the following week. Today was only Monday. Upon further questioning, he relayed the reason for such a long wait was trying to give his family from Georgia and Arkansas a chance to get to New York.

My Uncle Mack told him it was all well and good to think about the rest of his family but how disrespectful was it to keep Beemie on that cold slab for so long? He also told Griff if he had all the money for the services they should just proceed well before the following Friday. He tried to emphasize the fact that was almost a full two weeks and no one should be kept on ice for that long.

Griff said he understood and would discuss the matter with his mother. He also felt they would be a complete mess until his brother was laid to rest. He said he didn't want to see his brother go in the ground so the family decided to cremate him. They were not having a public viewing of the body. Only immediate family was allowed to see him before cremation. At the funeral would be his urn with his ashes instead of a coffin with his body. The urn would be adorned with lavender lilacs and a stand with pictures adorned with specially made black roses. Instead of holding the services at Ortiz Funeral Home on 149th street or McCall's on Bronx wood Avenue in the Bronx, the services would be held in the Ortiz Funeral Home on Sound view Avenue. It was away from the area and no chance of local thugs showing up since some traveling would be involved. The family wanted his final services to be held with some honor and decency.

The men gradually gravitated away from me to the side of the room and talked in hushed tones. It was out of my ear shot. I strained my neck to hear what was being spoken more clearly. They conferred on the revenge Griff was planning. He basically gave my uncle the full run down of the whole plan which was mapped out. He negated to tell my Uncle Mack it would be me who would more than likely dispose of the murder weapon.

My uncle hung on Griff's every word. He said he liked Griff's initiative and spunk. I overheard my uncle tell Griff there might be a spot open for him in his organization. He also told him the organization had branched out and secured a connection in Texas. Seems my uncle needed a young soldier he could trust to make the runs from New York to Texas. Once in Texas, the soldier was to meet the transnational gang La-Muerte which means the death.

La-Muerte and the soldier, preferably Griff, would then cross the border with the military style artillery and report to the Mexican cartel, Distribuidores de dolor. Distribuidores de dolor mean Dealers of Pain in English. They were ruthless however managed to stay under the authorities of Mexico and the United States radar. Due to this reason not too many people knew of them and those who did dared not whisper their name or they came up dead. Griff's face was very animated. His facial features registered looks of excitement, shock and anxiety.

My uncle explained further the workings of La-Muerte and Distribuidores de dolor. He said the group would have to stay at least four nights in Mexico. My Uncle Mack had an inside hook up with a Mexican woman he was courting named Marili. Marili was the assistant manager for a four star all-inclusive hotel about 8 miles away from Cancun. It was reasonably priced at two hundred and fifty nine dollars a night. I figured because it was only rated four stars. Despite the rating it was a main tourist attraction, clean and had a nice size pool area.

The group was to conduct business while having a little bit of pleasure. The layover was to avoid suspicion of constant crossing of the border even though my Uncle Mack had an inside contact for the border as well. He wanted the men to enjoy themselves. Marili would hire girls of the night as she called them but the old fashioned sensible word was prostitute for the guys. Upon hearing this my blood started to boil. I started rolling my eyes and talking under my breath. My Uncle Mack caught wind of my actions and screwed up his face. He pointed in my direction as if to ask Griff, "What's wrong with that child?"

Griff gave me a stern look and told my Uncle Mack everything was fine and it must be some sort of womanly mood swing or something. I wanted to take my shoe off and clunk him upside his head, if not before, I now paid attention. This time more intently to everything my Uncle had to say. It was bad enough I had to deal with Nakisha, Kiki, some loose ass squad members of mine and Lord knows whoever else fucking with Griff. I really didn't need any international floozy sucking on his dick as well. If Griff thought he was going to get off so easy and run down to Mexico just to do what I gave him privilege to do up here, he was sadly mistaken.

"Uncle Mack, I understand you got the game on smash when it come to the gun smuggling but what's up with the prostitutes? Your workers need to concentrate on the business at hand!" snidely I remarked trying to throw a monkey wrench in Griff's sick international hoe hunt.

"Never you mind niece. This is between me and the soldier Griff now. Why don't you get on in that kitchen and make your siblings some ravioli or Kool-Aid or something? I've been wondering how long you were going to ignore their cries of hunger," Mack's voice became very stern and harsh. He bent back and tried to peer down the hallway as if that would make him see through the wall into the bedrooms, "By the way where that old fish –eyed mama of yours? Does Angela always stay away this long? Does she have a job or something?"

"Oh, Lord, Uncle Mack, why you ask so many darn questions no one know where that crack head is at." If looks could kill I would have died a million deaths within a second.

"Don't you ever talk about your momma like that. You hear me chile? She may not be much but she the only parent you have. Do you know her burden's great? Her losing the one man who loved and never beat her; then having to deal with his damn momma, not even blood relation, taking jabs at her and interfering in their relationship. Once Leeq died, his momma dearest called Administration for Children's Services trying to have you all put in foster care. She wasn't even kin enough to take you herself. Good

thing Shaleeq stood his ground against his own
momma before he passed, when she told him to leave
Angela with retarded ass Junior and nappy headed ass
Eliza as she always called you by your first given
name. His momma said you didn't look like kin to her
no way and he should stay with Sasha's mother."

Uncle Mack abruptly stopped then stated, "Go on in
your room. I done went and said too much. Go on and
call the Chinese food place for you and the rest of the
children. I have to finish up this business. Speaking of
which, watch your fly ass mouth and stay out of
grown people business." He then opened his eyes
mad wide in expectation of my answer.

I simply stated, "Yes sir."

Walking away I couldn't help but think who the hell
Sasha was? Why did my uncle suddenly stop talking
when the name slipped out his mouth? Maybe Sasha
was a neighbor or something. Yet it seemed my King
Leeq was messing with this person's mother.

'Oh brother', I thought, 'How in the hell could this be
figured out?'

It was important in the sense I wanted to know every
detail I could about my father. Adoring him and
holding him to high esteem I would hate to think he
had any flaws. My father was superman to me;
Kryptonite temporarily destroyed his outer layer. This
only meant I knew death was the absence of the body.

Some people called it the shell. No matter what you chose to believe, his being was forever embedded in me. I mean my father was my world and I always was under the impression my mother got along with her in laws. I guess I was wrong. Shaking it off my brain waves and going into my mother's room instead of mine, I could hear them a little clearer.

I searched her cherry wood nightstand draws for the Chinese food menu. Moving the load of papers she had strewn in the drawers, I came across a brown paper bag filled with little baggies of crack. I immediately felt disgusted. Now I knew exactly where the money Uncle Mack was giving her bi-weekly was spent on. As I searched towards the back of the drawer my hand ran across what looked to be an EPT, pregnancy test. I was totally through, 'Hell no!' I screamed out loud. My mother had to be sadly mistaken if she thought I was helping her to raise any crack babies. She had four children she could hardly take care of now. What would she need with more? I gathered my emotions and came to the conclusion to discuss this matter with my mother when the right moment presented itself. For now I had to concentrate on the matter at hand which was to get some food in my younger siblings' stomach. After ordering two orders of half chicken, pork fried rice and egg rolls; I went back to trying to eavesdrop on my Uncle Mack and Griff's conversation.

My Uncle Mack was trying to impart knowledge as to why he ran his organization the way he did. He stated he felt if you were too much of a stickler or domineering your workers would soon resent you. Uncle Mack told Griff screw fear, resentment made the workers snitch on you since they wanted to be in your spot. A resentful person always neglected to take into account the hard work you put in to solidify your position. This person always wanted to take your place. They would somehow feel you weren't entitled to reap the benefits of your work and that they should be the head nigger in charge. He informed Griff this position called for days, if not weeks of being away from home. He asked Griff if this sounded like something he could handle.

"Yes sir, I sure can handle this position. It would really be my pleasure. Now with my baby bro gone, I am going to need some activities to take my mind off of his absence. If you don't mind me asking though sir, how much would you pay for my services?" Griff asked eager to make some real money.

Griff had an idea that gun trafficking could be lucrative but nearly fell out when my Uncle Mack said that newbies to the organization only received a base rate pay of one hundred and fifty thousand. The price, which was given, totaled a hundred and ten thousand more than Griff ever imagined. He quickly straightened up his face from the shock he felt and listened intently as my uncle droned on trying to sway him. In his mind Griff really didn't need to hear anymore because the prior number sealed the deal. My fast ass, however was taking notes. I didn't plan to be stuck in Mitchell Houses forever. Being the truant I am, also knew my elementary skills wouldn't get me very far.

Things were set in motion for Griff to become my Uncle Mack's new co-captain early next month. He was allowing Griff time to bury Beemie and grieve a little. Then my uncle brought up a subject I had long thought was going to go unpaid for.

"You know youngling, in my book there is an art to getting revenge. Take my situation in losing my heart, my half-brother Shaleeq. I know who and where the hit came from. Needless to say it's not what everyone thinks. I have since gained some pertinent information and I plan to show them my guns bark. However, I have bided my time. I don't want any leads pointing back to me when bodies start dropping. I might need to call you in on this revenge act as well. I am going to murder the person who put out the hit and the one who actually pulled the trigger. I say two more runs to Texas and Mexico and then I will be ready. If you accept, it would be a seventy-five thousand dollar payout for you. Can I count on you soldier?"

This really sparked my attention. It would be a fantasy come true if the man I was riding for avenged

my father's death. It got no sweeter than this. After a
few minutes, I realized Griff hadn't answered. My
heart beat raced with anticipation. I couldn't begin to
imagine why he would hold out. It would be the
sweetest seventy-five thousand dollar pay out.

"Sir, with all due respect, I need to focus on the
retaliation for my brother Beemie first. Afterwards, I
would have no problem helping you. I hope you are
okay with that?" he asked. His voice was a little
shaky. I was sort of upset at his response myself. I
wondered how you could tell the man who just
solidified your position in a crime organization which
had international ties and strongholds you had
something to do first. As I strained even more to
listen my cell phone started ringing. It was the
Chinese delivery man telling me he was downstairs
with the food. I told him to come up to my apartment
door and he said, "No door, lobby or no food."

He further infuriated me and I felt like leaving his ass
right there. I understand his hesitation. The local
thugs would call in to the Chinese restaurant and
place bogus orders. When the Chinese delivery man
arrived at the building and got on the elevator they
would then jump him. Nothing in his pockets was off
limits. If he had lint they were taking that as well.
Now as a precaution the delivery men would require
us to meet them in the lobby. Cursing him out and
telling him I would be right there all in one breath
decided to walk slowly so I could hear Uncle Mack's

verdict of Griff's slow acceptance to help him get revenge on our mutual enemies.

It seemed my Uncle Mack didn't take Griff's hesitation to heart as I did. I could hear him telling Griff don't worry he could wait just a little longer. In his waiting he expected Griff to have completed his path of destruction on his own course for revenge.

Just as I reached the living room the sight of my Uncle Mack giving Griff a man hug and telling him to hurry up and have Beemie's services brought tears to my eyes. These men were special to me and I was glad I brought them together. They both pulled apart and looked at me. I chuckled a little. All that talk my Uncle Mack was doing and now he is ashamed I saw him give someone a little affection.

"Don't mind me," I stated, "I am on my way to the lobby. Damn, chiney man scared to come upstairs. He act like I am going to rob him or something."

Griff let off a laugh and reminded me that I did once. I had to laugh myself at the memory. I was a rider in every sense of the word. I just hoped all my devious acts wouldn't catch up with me.

Chapter 5

Shatease and I rushed to get dressed. We were looking like the bopsy twins with similar black shirts and gray slacks and shoes. Our hair was similar to the night of the party. Shatease was acting a fool and didn't feel like messing with our heads. I really didn't want to spend the little money I made off the last shopping spree. Well theft spree actually, that we went on, to pay a salon for half assed work.

If my mother, Angela was really pregnant, I was going to need every dime I could get. I was young but it seemed like I was more responsible than my mother. Sometimes I had to take the benefit card, get the rent money and deliver it to the management office myself. Well at least before Welfare started sending the rent money directly to housing. It seems even with me paying the rent sometimes my mother managed to get us into a bind of threatened eviction. I really couldn't tell who the daughter was, her or me?

It was eleven thirty and the services started at twelve. Shatease and I rushed down stairs to the front of the building to try and catch a cab to Sound view. We got in a cab with an African man. He kept giving Shatease and me the 'eye' through the rear view mirror. I became so frustrated I had to say something. I asked him what the fuck he was looking at. He answered in some sort of broken English dialect, "No want no trouble," rambling on further, "you two just pretty."

"Yea, thanks. Just for future reference, I don't want any damn man who believe in having more than one wife," Shatease stated through clenched teeth. Her feelings were raw at the moment. It seemed like everything pissed her off. I gently patted her shoulder then laid my head on it.

"For real, for real," I cosigned, "now since you know she nor me fucking you turn your old ugly ass around and just drive. Or you won't get no damn cab fare motherfucker."

"I no want no trouble. Just pay please, I drive," he stated. I had to laugh. A motherfucker always changed their tune when you tell his ass they won't get any money.

Finally pulling up to the Funeral Home, I was happy Griff and his mother decided to move Beemie's services up to this Friday as opposed to waiting it out. There were some family members who were able to make the services. His mother was elated they did. A lot of people from the hood was upset there wasn't an actual viewing of the body. As for me viewing actual dead bodies freaked me out. Needless to say, I was happy about it.

I listened as Beemie's best friend read the eulogy. I was sort of amazed at the lies family and friends would sometimes tell of the dead. Then just chalked it up to them not wanting the family members, who didn't really know them, to think they were ghetto or something.

Some examples of the lies that were told pertained to Beemie's education and how generally nice of a person he was. Everyone from the hood knew Beemie was a motherfucking beast when it came to certain things he considered disrespectful. He had knocked many men teeth out of their mouths. Some were the local drunks who were known to frequent the bench area of the projects. The older local men who did every drug imaginable and fucked anything or crack head moving. I sometimes caught a few coming out my mother's room. Those are the ones I loved for Beemie to knock out. Especially since a couple of them gave me the creeps with the way they stared at me. One in particular tried to grab on my breast. When I told Beemie he beat him to a bloody pulp. Yes, Beemie was a true friend to me and I would really miss him.

Griff and Beemie's mother was a wreck. She was hysterically crying. Their mother wailed out sobs I heard once in church. It scared me then and it scares me now. Griff wasn't as hysterical as his mother. However, the tears flowed freely down his face. He didn't even bother to wipe them off his face.

Nakisha passed him some tissues and he smacked her hand away. 'Good,' I thought. How dare she get front row seat action with the family? I was the one who really knew Beemie. I was the one who chilled with him in the stairways and lobbies as we sold Griff's product. I was the one who looked out for the police coming up on his blind side. Most importantly besides being a co-conspirator with Beemie, I was the one satisfying Griff's oral pleasure and needs. How dare I have to sit in the back pews?

I was whispering violently in Shatease ear who indicated in more ways than one she did not want to hear it. I was so upset that my whispers became louder and an outcast of the family shushed me. I rolled my eyes at them and mouthed 'What?' Trust me if they were sitting in the back pew then they were no more important than me. The older lady sucked her teeth and turned her head forward. She kept it that way for the remainder of the services.

Shatease silently cried, sometimes to the point she lost her breath. I placed my arms around her and leaned in. I tried to tell her it was going to be alright but she just kept shaking her head and saying, "No, it's not."

The services were drawing to a close. The pastor officiating the service directed us on going up to the family to shake their hands and pay our respects. I dreaded this moment once I seen Nakisha in the front pews. I wanted to spit on her the same way she did me. When I reached up to the front, I bent down and whispered in Griff's ear, "You need to really dump chicken head and let me ease your pain." I then kissed him on his cheek and allowed my hand to linger on his knee. A look of disbelief was on his face but I knew he wouldn't make a scene. He firmly pushed my hand off his knee but not to the point where anyone would notice. I then rolled my eyes and giggled at Nakisha. She was a little bewildered yet stared back intensely. She didn't put any fear in my heart. She only intensified my anger. Trying to shake off the rage that I was feeling moved down the row to Griff and Beemie's mother.

I told her I was very sorry for her loss and softly kissed her on her forehead. I noticed her hair was graying slightly. I also informed her if there was anything at all she may have needed to never hesitate to inform me. She held my right hand in hers and then patted it, "Thank you so much sweetie. I appreciate your offer in my time of need. As for right now I am alright."

She then released my hand and took a tissue that Nakisha had passed her and dabbed at her nose. I cut my eyes at Nakisha again. This bitch is really pushing her luck. I was two seconds away from causing a holy rumble in the funeral home. I think Shatease sensed it because she quickly kissed Griff and Beemie's mother and grabbed me around my waist. She walked me out the funeral home. She then went to the main road and hailed for a cab while I started talking very animated and cursing. She turned around with daggers in her eyes. I'm not certain but I think she tried to kick her pink heels off which she changed into at the parlor.

"Bitch, if you don't change your tone and stop with your ole 'why me?' ass self, I am personally going to beat the brakes off you. Today, of all days, is not about you. Understand me. Today is the day I had to say good bye to my child's father," Shatease said shocking me to the core.

"Huh, baby Yannie is Beemie's daughter? Not Josh's? Damn, why you just telling me?" I was bewildered. I thought we were best friends how dare she not tell me something important like this?

"No, idiot, Yannie is Joshua's. I am pregnant. Two and a half months to be exact. Beemie is the father. His family doesn't know because I didn't get a chance to tell him. I really only found out a few days after he was murdered. I suspected it but was in denial. Once he died I took the test to be certain. I was thinking how nice it would be to have a piece of him, walking, talking and breathing.'

I was in a stupor. I didn't think her and Beemie was so serious. Then again getting information from Shatease was like pulling teeth if you didn't actually witness it. I ran to her and threw my arms around her.

I told her I was sorry for being such a self-centered jerk. The reality of what she was feeling and going through suddenly hit me. I bent down and started rubbing and talking to her belly.

"Hi pop-pop. It's auntie, who is also your god mommy, Koi. I am going to love you and spoil you like I do baby Yannie. I am going to go hard for you like you are my own."

Then I stepped back, did a little beat box sound with my mouth and started rapping. Positioning my hand like I had a mic the words I rapped were, 'We on top shooting those twin glocks nonstop and I am not tired. I have my twin glocks by my side and I bust my guns for life, I bust them for life. Those who don't know, soon realize. I bust till they loved ones die. They come hard, I come harder and our guns bust harder than theirs for life.'

Shatease was into it, shaking her head back and forth but then quickly cleared her throat and straightened out her clothes. I looked behind me and saw some of Griff's family members were walking out of the funeral home. Not wanting to be perceived as disrespectful for Shatease sake, decided to quit my performance. Shatease exhaled because I straightened up. She know sometimes I don't care about what people think of us. She finally was able to snag us a taxi and we went back to the block anxious to get out of our funeral attire.

We went in my room and I turned the laptop on. We started to undress looking for something more casual and comfortable to wear while it booted up. I chose some black cargo pants and a red shirt. On my feet I had some all black Jordan's with the gray jump man on the side. I plugged the flat iron in and giggled at Shatease who was deep in thought. I asked her why she was so quiet. What was on her mind? She said she wondered if it were time to quit smoking? Damn, I thought there goes my wake and bake buddy. Being selfish, I told her to wait until after this last cipher and then I told her to call Kemo. We needed at least six bags of weed for Beemie's memorial cipher. She did as I instructed while she rubbed her belly.

I logged onto my Face book page. There was nothing but Rest in Peace posts to Beemie and pictures from the funeral service. The pictures were hash tagged with a variety of quotes. The most popular one was #BeemiesWorld. Some of our friends made his picture from the funeral home their profile picture. We were definitely feeling the loss from Beemie's death. We congregated in the basketball court under the bridge by the highway and new building. Someone had an old time boom box which played cd's. They started playing some of Beemie's favorite songs. One in particular was Drake's 'Zero to a hundred'. We went wild screaming, 'Oh shit. Beemie spirit definitely here man!!'

We must have stayed in that basketball court for hours drinking, smoking, taking pictures for Face book and the gram, but most importantly telling stories about our favorite memories of Beemie. As we got ready to split up, I produced the nine my Uncle Mack gave me. I raised it high in the air and let off three rapid shots. After the last shot I screamed, "It's Beemie's World Playas." I looked around at the initial shock on everyone's face then it changed to recognition and a pleasant surprise as they started screaming 'Beemie's World Playas'. We all started doing Beemie's favorite dance the Shmurda dance.

After about thirty minutes of this we started to disperse. I got another one of my eerie feelings and pulled Shatease close to me. I looped our arms through each other's and slowed our pace so I can take in the scenery. I saw Griff and Mike come to blows with a dude from Rough Houser's squad. Not even thinking twice, Griff and Mike, jumped him. I ran to take part in the brutal assault as did Shatease. By this time the dude was on the floor getting kicked all over his body. Shatease was the first one of us females to touch him by kicking him square in the middle of his head. She must have hit him hard because his body started twitching. I pulled the nine out and aimed for the top of his head, "Let me put this nigger out of his misery!!! It's Beemie's World Playas."

I hesitated just a second and then fired. As the Rough Houser's skull bore open, I started crying. I didn't cry because I took a life; I cried because I just proved my loyalty for my heart Griff and his family. I thought for sure now he would love me more than Nakisha. I technically committed the first act of revenge for Beemie. My hand shook as I lowered the weapon. Griff was beside me trying to take the gun. He whispered in my ear after kissing the side of my face very tenderly, "Now that's gangster."

My heart was overjoyed by his validation. That particular night there wasn't any rented friend's room or rooftop rendezvous. He paid for a motel stay and was finally able to penetrate me. It hurt at first but then I got into it. I rode him backwards and everything. He manhandled me a little by flipping me around, doing it doggy style, smacking my ass and roughly shoving his dick in my mouth. I don't even recall how many times or what positions we fucked in. All I l know is my man can now say he made a woman out of me. Griff may not have known at the moment but I was going to be riding shotgun on his gun smuggling assignments. This just made sense. I proved I was loyal and down to commit homicide for him. I planned to tell him after he found out the exact date of his initial assignment and it would be war if he denied me the chance of accompanying him at least on this assignment.

After check out time we went over the bridge which
connected the Bronx to Mount Vernon and ate at
IHOP. He ordered steak and eggs. It came with two
pancakes and unlimited cups of coffee. Perusing the
menu, I decided to sort of be a follower and get the
country friend steak and eggs. It was accompanied by
all of the same sides as Griff's. The only difference
was I had a sort of white gravy. I was so hungry and
borderline dehydrated, I believe I felt every thud as
the bites of food hit my hollow stomach. Besides the
Chinese food Uncle Mack made me order I hardly
could remember what exactly I ate. Signaling for the
waiter to come over, I asked for a tall glass of ice
water. Upon its arrival I gulped the contents of the
glass down and began to chomp on the ice. Griff
instantly became frustrated.

"Yo, I know this is not a five star, gourmet restaurant
but can you act like you have some home training?"

"Fuck you talking about bae?" I asked a little
stumped. I was a little rough around the edges but
didn't think I looked that bad. Also if he could feel
how I felt he would be asking for even more water to
give to me.

"I'm saying, just be easy. There's no need to act like
a hood rat, chewing on ice and shit. Sip your water
and set the glass down without all the extra stuff. You
doing too much. Got it?"

We had a wonderful night and in not wanting to ruin it I came to the conclusion of not arguing with him. "Got it; loud and clear bae," I told him. I put a smile on my face and patted him gently on his hand. "I need to talk to you bae."

"Yea, what about, wait, don't tell me cuz it's too early to tell if you are pregnant or not."

He then fell out in a fit of laughter. I felt it wasn't that funny. Then the truth of Shatease situation fell from my lips. "No silly, but you going to be an uncle. Are you excited?"

I waited for his response but he only sat there looking perplexed.

"What, you fucked Beemie? I don't find this very funny Koi. You know I lost my heartbeat. You supposed to be my chick and you fucked my brother?"

"No, silly you know my ass was a virgin until last night. What I am saying is Sha-Sha is going to be Beemie baby mother. She just doesn't know how to tell the family. I figured I would help her out by letting you know. Aren't you happy?"

A cloudy gaze came instantly over his eyes as he stared me in mine. I caught the shivers. I really didn't understand what his hesitation or unhappiness was about. It was almost spooky. In all the lifetime movies I watched with my mother the same look came over the abusive husband or killer eyes. It was so intense I thought he was going to reach across the table and choke me out. However, when he opened his mouth it was totally not what I initially expected.

"Hmm, I see. Let me be real about a few things. Number one given Shatease history, how do I know the baby is really my brother's? It's not like she was his girl or something."

This wasn't what I thought would happen when the bright idea popped in my head to spill the beans. The magnitude of the truth of his words really hit me. I didn't want to doubt my Day One but they did keep their relationship, or whatever it was, under wraps. Despite this little nagging doubt, I decided to plead her case since I honestly thought Beemie was the baby's father.

"Well Griff, I don't think Shatease would appreciate you saying all this about the baby's father. We both weren't there when they were fucking so I am operating off the assumption you are the uncle."

"You know what happens when you assume. Do I have to explain it to your ghetto ass again? All I am saying is IF, and that is a big IF, Beemie is the father my family will help her take care of the baby, If not she can kick rocks. I told Beemie to stop trying to wife up chicks from the same hood. It's not a good look."

"Oh so you saying you would never wife me?" I was now upset by the advice he once gave to his deceased brother. If I read in between the lines, it would only tell me that Griff didn't see himself having a future with me. How was I supposed to digest this new discovery?

The food was served and we dug in. The silence between us was deafening. The tension between us was so thick it would take a samurai's knife to slice it. I looked up and Griff had a funny look on his face. I smirked some and asked him why he was looking at me like that. He stated there were some things about Shatease I didn't know. When I asked him to elaborate he said he would let me find out for myself but in the meantime he questioned her loyalty to our friendship.

If Griff had made those statements about one of my other friends I would have taken his word as bond. However, because it was Shatease I brushed it off to him losing his brother. I mainly figured he had mixed feelings about the baby she was carrying so his emotions were kind of raw. Not bothering to continue beating a dead horse, I concentrated on my food. The food was good but due to my current mind frame I really couldn't enjoy it. I forced myself to eat the rest then finally brought up my idea about Texas and Mexico to Griff.

"Bae, I don't know how you would feel about this. I was thinking of accompanying you on your first run to Texas. I just don't want you going by yourself and figured you needed one of your home team players to go with you. Trust me you won't even know I will be there. I am going to just ride shotgun, while holding you down if you need me to."

I stopped talking before I said too much and waited anxiously for his reply.

"Really?" he burst out laughing then gaining his composure he started talking, "Now, doesn't your uncle have people on the payroll to accompany me to these locations? Really Koi, I know it has to be something more than what you are saying. Spill it and I might just think about it."

Not wanting to tell him the real reason was so he couldn't be influenced to sleep with prostitutes, I simply told him after everything that happened with Beemie and our first real intercourse experience I think it would be hard to be separated from him right now. I became misty eyed and had to hold back tears that were threatening to fall from my eyes.

He simply looked at me and nodded his head. A few more minutes went by and he signaled for the waiter to bring the check. He looked at me as the waiter went to get his change for a hundred dollar bill.

"Koi, I don't know how you plan to stay gone so long from your family. Do you know how much your mother relies on you? She damn near needs you for everything. I would love for you to come the more I think about, it but what would your Uncle say? How do you propose we get away with that?" He asked some very pertinent questions. I really didn't think things through but knew I would come up with something. I wanted to be with him on this trip first time out.

I needed to scope out the workings of my Uncle's operation as well. I had plans to oversee things when I was older. Uncle Mack really didn't have any children. Who would he leave everything to? I should be the next in line because Junior was disabled. Speaking of which, I had to talk to my mother about his social security check.

I have been noticing lately she hasn't bought any new linen or even clothes for my younger siblings. My mother would usually take my younger sister to get her hair washed and set at the hairdresser on Westchester Avenue. I believe it had been about two months since they last went. Junior's check and the biweekly payouts from Uncle Mack should have been enough to keep all our beauty and hygiene needs in check along with some food and things for the house.

It then hit me. I could get in her ass and cause a big fight. I would do this around the time of Griff's first run. It would be the perfect excuse. I could tell my Uncle my mother was back on crack and I found out she owed a lot of money to the crack man. In this revelation, we fought and she put me out the house. Knowing my mother it wasn't too big of a stretch.

I told Griff of my plan and he agreed it could work. I was elated. Soon I would be on the road with my love. I was secretly salivating over the fact Nakisha could never tag along on this. I was Griff's go to girl and that was better than a wife if you asked me. I spent more time with 'Our Man' and he confided in me more. She may have provided him monetary security but I provided him physical security. Which one was more important? I already proved I would bust my gun from Griff and our squad. I also gave him the hook up with a guns dealer. I mean if he was alive and well armed he could make money but if he was dead all she could do was bury him with her money. Who's to say she would do anything once he was gone? I would be fifteen soon and we were already fucking. I wasn't a little girl with just a crush on him anymore. I believed we had something solid. He just needed to wake the fuck up and focus on seeing that. In the meantime, I was going to play my position until my actions solidified my spot in his life.

Chapter 6

We had one week before it was time to leave and travel to Texas. Griff called an emergency meeting of us soldiers and riders. He said things for him wouldn't feel somewhat normal until he murdered the actual person who was the cause for his brother's brutal killing. He reiterated our plan and passed out positions to the participants.

I was somewhat happy to see Fuquan, whom I haven't seen since the night of the party. A lot had changed including my feelings for him. At least that was what I initially thought before I seen him. When the roles went out it was disclosed he was actually messing with William's sister Sassy. He was going to use the fact William and his family hadn't paid rent in the last four months. Fuquan said he can get William to meet him at the management office under the pretense he would pay the families back rent. He also informed us William didn't really know what was being planned but did speak on the need to watch his back. William also told Fuquan he was going to stay strapped at all times and walk with more than one Rough Houser. Trying to be hard he told Fuquan these steps were all precautions in case something popped off with Griff and his men. Fuquan knew it was all a front of sorts and William didn't have the heart to actually face Griff. He knew William put the word out and had the Rough Houser's handle the dirt he wished he was capable of handling. Fuquan said once they reached the management office he would send a text to the shooter who would be waiting in the car. The car was to drive by and bust shots at William only when Fuquan was safely out the way. Fuquan said to make sure everything was followed to the letter because all though he was brave he didn't want to feel any hot lead on his body. He said he been down that road before and wasn't willing to go down it again. The rehabilitation time was too much and he had to grind for his money. He had a household to support. I rolled my eyes thinking, 'Didn't we all?'

We all believed this would work fine as long as we stuck to the script. I couldn't tell a lie though I was upset he was messing around with Sassy. Sassy was pretty for an average type chick. She was into her schooling so I was sort of surprised she was messing with Fuquan. Her family was just as poor as mine. However, unlike me she wasn't a hustler. I think she was trying to step her game up in dealing with Fuquan. I bumped into him on purpose and then whispered in his ear casually it was nice to see him. He looked at me with a sparkle in his eyes and a smirk on his mouth. He got ready to say something but then Griff interrupted. "You two look engrossed; hmm, I wouldn't say cozy but damn near close to it. Everything all right here?"

Griff's tone was a little unsettling. I thought to myself he must really love me to show a little bit of jealousy of me talking to another male. His actions gave me some hope he would leave Nakisha and be with me. The thoughts of advice he last gave to his brother popped in my head. It might be a long shot but his actions now were showing me there was a chance he would do just that. I figured all would be revealed through his actions on the trip to Texas.

In my mind I was just talking to Fuquan but Griff saw it differently. He noticed Fuquan's hand around my waist and the smile on my face. I all but thought I was over any chemistry for Fuquan. Griff must have sensed some uncertainty on my part regarding if it was really over between Fuquan and I. He came to the conclusion to end it before it started. He told Fuquan to set everything in motion for two days and we would see him then. He put his arm around my neck and then casually but very roughly drew me to him. He damn near dragged me out the front door.

"What is it between you and that nigga? You two are always in each other's faces. If you two are fucking you might as well tell me now. Don't have me looking stupid like your play 'cousin' Shatease had my brother. You can damn sure tell me, I will leave your little ass alone. Speaking of Shatease, Ma Dukes and I want a DNA test."

I really didn't know what he meant about Shatease and Beemie. Judging from her reaction the other day at his funeral they were in a committed relationship. Now here was Griff insinuating something different. I hated when people did that. I wished everyone would be the adult their ages said they were and speak the truth that is on their mind. I was the youngest out of every squad I ran or casually hung with yet I acted most mature. It was sickening and I realized since the age of five when I lost my father, I have always had to play the role of adult. As far as the request for a DNA test I was sort of taken aback. The old but familiar saying, 'Mama's baby, Papa's maybe' jumped into my head.

"How do you suppose we do that? Your brother is gone remember? Fuck you going to do take her and embarrass yourselves on Maury or something?" I was becoming upset. This wasn't going the way I expected. Maybe I shouldn't have opened my mouth. Maybe I should have let her handle it but I doubt she would have. Shatease had expressed in a separate conversation she didn't want to go through similar situations that she went through with baby Yannie's father. Due to this reason, she may not inform Griff and his mother about the baby she was pregnant with. I felt in telling Griff it would open up the door and make it easier for her to have a line of communication with Beemie's family. Now at the end of the day I guess I was wrong. I hated to have to be the one to tell Shatease. I asked Griff to keep it a secret until she divulged the information herself. He looked at me and giggled.

"Sure, why not? Your 'play cousin' don't tell you everything anyway. All I know is when the baby get here she better consent to DNA testing if she expects a dime from me."

Griff kept laughing. My blood was boiling now and I was tired of him calling Shatease my play cousin'. I opened up my mouth to tell him just as much.

"Why are you clowning? Every other line out your mouth is calling Sha-Sha my 'play cousin'. What's up with that? Also, why are you saying she keeping secrets from me. I am pretty sure she tell me everything. Stop bugging out and just be prepared to swallow some of your words as soon as my little man gets here."

"Trust me Koi, I wish I could tell you right now but I think it's better to sit it out and see if your play...I mean best friend is going to keep it a hundred with you."

I came to the conclusion to just let him talk. We had bigger things to do like getting ready to retaliate against Beemie's murderers and getting ready to go to Texas. Speaking of which, I kissed Griff hard and passionately on his mouth taking him by surprise. He stuck his tongue in my mouth and put his hand down my shirt. We stood locked like that for a moment until we heard someone beefing at us.

"Now isn't this about some shit? Fuck you all up on this young bitch. What happened Griff? Where's all that fly talk when I asked you if the two of yawl were more than friends; all the denials? You were swearing up and down she was just some little teen whose mother was out there so you looked out for her. You were swearing on your dead daddy that she was too young for you and you would never violate anyone's trust like that. What happened to my trust?"

By now Nakisha was up in his face pushing him on the shoulder. Tears were streaming down her eyes as she started trying to mush him in the head, "I guess I am too old to be your girl. I don't do the side chick thing. It's all or nothing with me. You standing out in public on a corner, kissing a 13 year old. Huh? You disgust me?"

"Bitch, I am fourteen and some change. I will be fifteen before he even see twenty. Fuck you mean too young?"

As I droned on trying to draw her attention away from him so I could put the paws on her, she looked totally spaced out and seemed to be ignoring me. I wrapped my arms around Griff's waist and pulled him in closer to me as if to say you can't have him and that is when Nakisha turned all focus on me.

"Aww, you young bitch!" She came racing towards me with her claws out. Her hands looked perched like bird claws. Just like I figured she wasn't really a scrapping type of bitch. She fought like a girl who only scratched and pulled hair. I didn't put much stock into this fight. As a matter of fact I played with her a little. I bobbed and weaved all over that broad. She would stop, huff and puff, perch her claws and run after me again. I would side step her every time, and mush her in the back of her head. Being long winded and probably embarrassed more than anything, she bent over and put her hands on her knees. She took long gasps of air. Finally, she let out a deep low hollow scream, ran and clunked Griff in his head. I stood in my fighter's stance thinking she was going to come after me again. However, I think she knew better. She kept trying to clunk him upside the head and he kept swatting her away; just not as rough as me. I laughed at them and stood back as a group started to form. They watched the show Nakisha was putting on while Griff tried to refrain himself from knocking the bitch out. Then all of a sudden, when embarrassment set in he reached out and grabbed her by the neck. She looked like a chicken getting strangled and all you heard from the crowd were, "oohs and ahhs and oh shit's".

Some men who I have seen around the way watched intently whispering to each other. I then heard one say,

"Naw man, he can't be manhandling that lady. He fucking her up."

Me being the little rebel rouser I was responded back to him. "And what the fuck you gone do about it?"

Feeling called out and his manhood tested, tried to defend Nakisha's honor by grabbing the hand Griff used to strangle her. Griff caught him square on the jaw with a crossover from his free hand and threw Nakisha to the floor. I walked over and spit on her, "Spittle for spittle you old ass bitch. He don't want that old worn out shit you call a pussy. Looking like some old raw dog meat and smelling like cabbage, He want this tender youngling you can never be again."

The crowd was a little disgusted by the whole display and started to disperse with the exception of those who wanted to see the so called hero get his ass kicked. I remembered dude came with a friend and scanned the stragglers for him. I spotted him making his way toward me and Nakisha. I got back in my fighting stance in case I had to go toe to toe with old dude but instead he reached his hand down to assist Nakisha off the ground who was whimpering like a hurt puppy. I rolled my eyes at captain save a hoe and watched Griff place one final blow on the hero's bridge of the nose which somehow knocked him out. I was in all my glory knowing my dude was gangster and I was bout it as well. He looked at Nakisha and told her he was disgusted by her. She was always flipping out, nagging him and causing a scene. He told her don't call him until she got her shit together. His next words though broke my heart and solidified my decision to leave him after the trip to Texas.

"You can't just beat up on every female who works for me. Get some self- esteem about yourself." He looked at me then continued, "Go ahead home, start packing for your o.t. trip. I will call you about the other situation after I get her situated in a cab to queens."

Not being able to really contain myself, but not wanting to play the role of fool anymore in front of these stragglers asked him, "Are you serious about yourself right now? 'Go ahead home until that bitch is situated, Yea a'ight."

I picked my face and feelings up off the floor and went on about my business. I called Kemo and copped four bags of weed. I would have called Shatease but I needed to get dopey by myself. I went into my mother's prescription stash and found two Percocet's. I popped one and washed it down with the Cisco I sent the neighborhood bum into the liquor store to get. I had to pay him two dollars. The peach Cisco was my shit. I remember my mother caught me drinking it once and took the bottle from me. Just when I thought she was going to scream at me as any rational, sober mother would do, she turned the bottle up to her mouth and took a long ass sip. She looked at me and said, "Ahhh, liquid crack! This was me and your father's shit back in the days. This is how I became pregnant with your big head brother Junior. Liquid crack and mess tabs."

My mother fell out laughing and I felt disgusted. I snatched my bottle of Cisco back and screamed at her, "Give me my shit! Fuck you! You think everything is a joke?"

I wiped the top of the bottle off with my shirt. As many dicks as my mother sucked wasn't any telling what type of germs she had. She rolled her eyes but didn't say too much. She just huffed and puffed about who had who and how I better show her some respect before she put the paws on me. At that time I was only testing my mother I would not think of hitting her back. It wasn't until she stole my siblings Christmas presents that sent me over the edge.

I chuckled to myself at the memories of my first drink or attempt of getting tipsy. While I enjoyed my reveries, I continued drinking my Cisco while rolling up my weed. Instead of rolling it fine and thin like I usually did, I rolled a monster blunt. The damn white owl tore a little so I had to use more spit than I was used to. I think it was my nerves of getting played out by Griff in front of Nakisha that had me on edge. I was tired of it and I thought since we actually had sexual intercourse and not only oral sex things had changed. I was sadly mistaken.

I lit the blunt and inhaled deeply. I took in the sweet aroma of the burning weed as the tears slid silently down my face. I let them flow freely. I couldn't wait to get this road trip over. Afterwards, Griff was losing me, his ride or die. I was still young and going to move on. I was going to find someone who admired and cherished the gem that was me and all that I offered. Regardless, to the fact if I was young or not I had feelings and Griff stepped on them for the last motherfucking time and that was word to my King Shaleeq.

Chapter 7

I fell asleep laying across my bed, with the blunt in
my mouth. I actually was awoken by my mother
screaming that I had burned the mattress. I checked
my cell phone while she was in my room chastising
me.

There was a message from Griff explaining Nakisha
was in bad shape emotionally but I should just keep
packing. He was also moving the retaliation for
Beemie's murder up. It seemed my Uncle needed him
to make the trip to Texas sooner than planned. He
wanted me and Shatease ready at the drop of a hat. He
also said to get the plan with my mother in motion
and to also tap her ass if I had to. Griff said he needed
me desperately to go with him. He said he knew I was
upset for the lies he told Nakisha. The message ended
and I rolled over unto my back and stretched while
looking at the ivory white ceiling. I then focused on
my mother still yapping and I moved in for the attack.

Getting off the bed and circling around her I asked
her what the fuck she was doing with a pregnancy test

in her drawer. She stopped folding my pink taffeta blanket and looked me dead in my eyes.

"Why the FUCK you going through my belongings? And who the FUCK are you to be questioning me? I am getting real tired of your mouth and actions young lady. There's going to be some changes around here seriously."

My mother moved around me and grabbed the broom. She bent down and began sweeping under my twin sized bed. My room was neat compared to the rest of the house but she still managed to bitch and moan about some blunt shavings on the floor.

"You're a fine one to talk, used condoms, chicken bones and crack vials in your room out in plain sight! Did you forget you had children? Thank God Shaleeq is our father or we would be even more screwed up with just you and one of your crack head partners!"

I was up in her face, yelling and screaming. My right pointer finger was poking her in the shoulder. My mother had me by a few inches as far as height was concerned but I wasn't scared of her. My embarrassment and anger from Griff's actions was bubbling over. Angela, my mother was going to feel the wrath of my storm. I must have poked her too hard because she slapped my hand away.

I yelled at her, "Bitch, don't touch me."

I mushed my mother in her forehead so hard her head snapped back. She looked dazed but snapped out of it. She caught me with a left hand open slap to the side of my face. Before I knew it I had both my hands around her neck and I was squeezing as if my life depended on it. My mother was by no means a slouch and her animalistic instincts kicked in once I pushed her roughly against the wall. She clutched her fist tightly closed and pummeled me on the side of my head. We tangled with each other for what seemed like eternity until Junior ran in the room and started screaming in his awkward tone. He grabbed both sides of his head and stomped his feet. I became nervous as I never seen him do these things before. My mother took this opportunity and punched me square in my mouth. My entire right side of my lip swelled up and split.

I was horrified. She started poking me back and telling me to get out of her house. I swatted her hand away yelling back at her that I needed to pack my stuff.

"Bitch fuck that shit. Go steal you some more fucking rags, you little thief. You think I care about this shit?"

She started scooping my clothes up from the sorted laundry pile in the middle of the floor and rushed toward the window. I screamed for her to stop and put them back. She turned around, looked at me and said, "Or what?"

I was temporarily lost, frozen in time without a snazzy comeback. I don't think this is what Griff had in mind when he told me to tap her ass if need be. All I could muster was a 'you'll see'.

She laughed out loud and made a mad dash for the window and threw the load in her arms out the window. She turned back around and laughed, "Oops, did I do that?" she chuckled very evil like and then added, "Or what now?"

She shrugged her shoulders when I didn't respond fast enough and bumped her way passed me. "It's 2:45pm. You have exactly an hour to get the fuck out my house. Oh yes, before I forget your man Griff and best friend Sha-Sha send their regards."

She sashayed out the door leaving me there looking crazy. For the life of me I couldn't figure out what she meant by bringing up the two people I was most close to.

Figuring I better hurry up, I left the rest of the clothes on the floor. I went for my stash of stolen blank prescription papers in between my mattress and box spring. I had to find a way to get them filled. I also decided, I could boost any material item I needed. Then on second thought I shouldn't have to since Griff would be rolling in the dough from this trip to Texas.

I sat on the edge of my bed and held my head in my hands. Feeling a little flustered, wondered how I was going to face Griff with this busted lip. I was praying my eyes weren't bruised as well.

Instantly thinking of Nakisha I whispered to myself karma's a bitch. I planned to make up with my mother after my trip with Griff. It is not like I had anywhere else to go anyway. I also couldn't leave my siblings in this house with our crack head of a mother for too long either. She was trying to act right because of her pregnancy but who says she was going to keep it anyway.

Amidst my thoughts, I heard banging on the front door. It was Shatease, Milk, Mike and Bam. I overheard my mother saying, "Yea, the little bitch is in her room. Well, her old room. I am putting her out. Fuck a system. She done put her hands on me for the last time. Let her fend for herself the best way she knows how. Next time the little hoe touch me, I am going to take a bat after her. Dumb ass child of mine should have been born smarter. I swear she don't have a brain anything like me or Leeq. What a natural shame; she pretty, but dumb at the same time. If she was white her hair would be blonde."

Then I heard my mother mumbling under her breath and walk mad fast to her room. Slamming the door, I swear she put her face in the pillow and screamed. I heard flicks of the lighter which indicated to me she had the crack stem and was taking some hits. Two seconds later she was back bothering Shatease to go on and tell me something. There were hushed tones and Shatease telling my mother to please don't do that. She was asking my mother why she couldn't leave well enough alone.

I heard my mother say if you don't tell her I will and how dare Shatease let Bianca, her own mother take the blame for Baby Yannie having her own crack pipe? Shatease started crying and my mother then turned to the guys and said, "Yawl know I am not the only crack hoe around here. I done saw her plenty of times in that place you call a trap house. Now she either tells Koi or I will. She and Bianca think they are so fly and better than everyone else. However, they just as fucked up and dysfunctional as the rest of us."

My leg went to shaking and I couldn't hold it any longer. I flew out my room and asked everyone what the fuck was all this going on in my living room? I stood in the middle of the living room pointing and hollering that if anyone had something to tell me they might as well do it now. Everyone looked at me all bug eyed then looked at Shatease. For the first time I saw fear and knew that whatever came next would be deep. At that point I believed I didn't even want to know. I wanted things to stay as they were between us. I had lost my King Shaleeq to gun violence, my mother to drugs and now from what I could tell, I was about to lose the only other person I ever trusted besides myself. I don't remember much after that because all I know is I blacked out after my mother said, "That pregnancy test is hers but what you don't know is she wasn't sleeping with only Beemie but Griff as well. See, I am not the only crack smoking hoe in this room."

I looked at Shatease and Griff's hesitation about accepting the baby as a nephew or niece started to make sense, his insistence of her taking a DNA test. I would not show weakness even though I wanted to cry. I simply asked her, "Is this true? Have you been fucking Griff as well?"

Shatease hesitation and stuttering were enough to send me over the edge and I blacked out.

After snapping out of my blackout, I realized some of Shatease hair was halfway out of her head, her eye was swollen shut and her nose was leaking blood like a water fountain. She was blubbering like a five year old child who couldn't get what they wanted in a grocery store or candy aisle.

"Koi, I am sorry. I mean it wasn't like I was fucking him with the intentions of being his girl or anything. It happened once or maybe twice. There were no feelings involved what so ever."

"No, feelings involved you say? Tell me Sha, what am I? Do I not have feelings? Why do I feel this way, great, chopped liver! That is all I am to anybody.

Well, fuck all this dumb shit before I really fuck shit up, just for future reference stay the fuck away and don't speak to me when you see me. As far as baby Yannie, I feel sorry for her. She have a married, white daddy who don't want any parts of her and a hoe ass, crack head for a mother and grandmother. The odds are stacked against all of yawl because you all lost the one common denominator in your pitiful lives," I then pointed to myself making certain to point to my heart, "Me!" then I turned and went back to my room. I grabbed my blank prescription papers and cell phone from off my bed, went to the far corner of the room and kissed my siblings who were sitting on their Oak wood bunk beds. They all had tears in their eyes and the two verbal youngsters asked me to stay and not go. Junior grabbed my arm and put his head on my shoulder. He stomped his feet again. I was going to miss them but needed to get away. I didn't know how much more I could take. I wasn't too sure what I was going to do about Griff. I do know that I needed whatever money this trip to Texas would make.

"God," I cried out loud, "What is a girl to do? Where are all the people who supposed to be there for me?"

I pushed Junior off me, walked into the living room and stormed passed the circle of so called friends and family members who were supposed to have my back like I had theirs. Slamming the door behind me I jogged to the staircase exit and as I pushed the door Mike came out behind me.

[109]

"Koi, wait up," he yelled. I turned around and rolled my eyes. I don't know what part he had in Shatease and Griff fucking, if he had any. I wasn't too sure I wanted to know the details of his involvement as well. I needed for someone to be on my side for once. I needed someone who was unbiased yet experienced enough to know my struggle. The feelings I were going through was making me a wreck but I needed an insider who could tell me the next move I should make.

"What up?" I said turning around slightly aggravated. Wiping the tears from my eyes with the back of my hand I shrugged my shoulders for lack of anything better to do, "Please don't tell me you have more revelations for me. I really do not know what else I am supposed to hear that is not going to push me over the edge. Please if it's going to hurt my feelings don't bother to even tell me. I really don't think I should care anymore."

"Koi, when have you ever known me to gossip? In all truthfulness, I cannot speak on those things which I know nothing about." I felt a little better hearing this from him. Even if it wasn't true I wanted to have an ally. Someone who was just as clueless as me is what my self-esteem and betrayed heart required.

Mike continued, "I know you are hurt right now. You feel like you have been betrayed by your friend and who YOU consider to be your man. However, if not mistaken, I told your young ass before, this is just puppy love. You can't possibly have or tame a man who belongs to anyone else. He does have his wifey and you know that. Now, I am not going to beat you up about it. You're my little soldier. You will get over this. I just need to be sure you can separate business from pleasure. I am going to still need you to get out your bag of feelings and hold us down like I know you can. The only thing I can do is make sure that Shatease isn't any longer a part of this plan but you still have to deal with Griff. So, I know I have no right to ask you. But can you please not bring up what happened just now until after William and his crew is done for? I just need Griff's whole attention on this. I don't need any slip ups. Got me?"

I looked at him like he had ten heads. I was livid. In a way he had a right. Beemie was my boy as well. We did share some good times. I could have been with Beemie when he got murdered and for that William and his squad needed to pay.

We had to stick together as a unit when it came to street things but I was an individual dealing with matters of the heart. I realized I really didn't have anywhere to stay. I told Mike until they were ready to put this work in tonight I would be chilling at Mercedes house. He said it was going to go down in about two hours so he don't care where I went as long as I was around then. Just like I figured everyone always need me for their purpose and then I am discarded.

"Yea, understood. Oh, for this mission I don't need to see Griff so please try to keep him away from me," I testily stated. Mike sucked his teeth and rolled his eyes and then stated,

"You need to really come to the conclusion if you want Griff in your life as you being only the side chick or fuck buddy or if you want him to help you stack paper and keep your pockets on swole. It seems to me you are not going to let the two things be separate factors in your life. A disagreement in one aspect of you two relationship will greatly affect the other. There is more than just Griff and me needing you to come through on your end, there is a whole team of players. Now imagine how Milk and Bam feel after seeing all this shit? Do you think they feel safe knowing how emotional you are? You are a live wire. I don't care about Griff fucking my girl, my friend or my cousin as long as he not fucking Ma dukes aka Grandma or my baby sisters I am good. You need to decide what's good for you and in what capacity. Now on that note I am gone."

Mike made an about face and left me standing there in the hallway staring at his back. Halfway down the hall he turned around and said, "Be ready in two hours. You know the drill, Management Office on

143rd street heifer. Don't make me come looking for you if you not there on time got it?"

"Yes, Management Office on 143rd at ten in the night got it. I am going to go to Cedes (my nickname for Mercedes), smoke a blunt and chillax for a minute. Thanks again Mike for the talk. You could have just let me go and talked about me like a little bitch with the others. Glad to see you came to school me on some things. I believe after the Texas trip, I am going to just deal with Griff on a business level. I'm too young and lost everyone I loved already. I might as well just roll for self-whole heartedly."

Mike looked at me and nodded his head. He turned back around and went back in my house. It was weird having to leave everyone there knowing I may not ever return. As for Shatease, I was angry but not with her. I was just angry at her ways yet still loved her. It stuck me like a knife in my heart that I actually had no one left. I had no pops, no moms, no best friend and especially no man. Who was going to hold me the way I needed to be or loved me the way I needed to be and yes, who was going to fuck and suck me the way I needed to be. It damn sure wasn't going to be Griff.

Who would it be remained to be seen? I did, though, have an idea. I just had to see how things played out after this revenge hit and trip to the lone state. In the meantime, I hustled my ass down the stairs, ran across the big ass street and ran into the burger joint. I ordered a bacon cheeseburger with onion rings and told them to put the pickles on the side. After five minutes, I told the counter boy to give me a large double chocolate shake. I was hoping it would help chase the blues away. I grabbed my order when it was ready and headed to Millbrook Houses. I hoped I didn't see Steph. She was my longtime enemy who talked too much. The last thing I needed was another confrontation. I made it to 584 without incident and made a left once I entered the lobby.

Mercedes was an older lady who boosted as well. She was the one who taught Shatease and me some of the art form of boosting. She lived on the first floor in a studio apartment. She had a pullout sofa I would be able to sleep on. She was anal when it came to cleaning. I mean she didn't like anything out of place and would even clean behind you after you used the toilet. She would always say the doctors told her she had OCD. Mercedes said she didn't agree but only felt why let the germs fester. That is how you bred germs. I really didn't get it only said I did and left it at that.

I knocked in my usual code. After what seemed like forever, I heard her saying 'Oh shit!' and then she told me to hold on a minute. I heard the spritz of an air freshener can spraying. Rolling my eyes I wondered why I just didn't call my Uncle Mack to come pick me up. I came to the conclusion I would deal with the drug addict for a couple of days. I really had to take stock of my life. I would be only fifteen soon but I lived a harsh life already. When Shaleeq died all childhood died with him. This was my reality and enough to give anyone nightmares for life. I took a deep sigh and realized my food was getting cold so I banged on her door and told her to hurry the fuck up. I heard the shuffle of her slippers and then the door flung open, "Hold your horses little bit."

"Fuck you mean, 'hold my horses?' If you only knew the horrible night I had you would be flying to open the door plus do anything that I needed done." I said exasperated.

My eyes became misty again. Cedes told me to take a chill pill and go sit in the living area while she tidied up the bathroom real fast. I took the door and slammed it shut and told her to fuck all that. I needed an honest answer and I needed it soon as I only had one hour and thirty minutes to spare. I had business to take care of.

She jumped back and said, "All right, all right, don't get your panties in a bunch."

Mercedes put the chain lock on and moved back into the living area. She turned on her computer and windows media player opened up to the sensual voice of Aaliyah, singing 'I care for you.'

I felt like crying in that moment. It was my mother's favorite jam. She played this song ever since I could remember. I wished she could become healthy by kicking this drug habit. I longed for the mother who washed and braided my hair or twisted it with little colorful clips on the end to match each outfit I wore. The one who would put me on a pillow lay me across her lap and rock her legs back and forth when I cried too much. She knew exactly how to sooth me. Now it seemed my mother didn't know me enough. I asked Mercedes to change the song. She could tell by the look on my face that she better. She put on the Nikki Minaj and Ariana Grande song and I felt a little more at ease. I explained to her the happenings of today without really getting into the detail of why I spazzed out on my mother. Mercedes the ever philosophical soul said that my mother needed to move past grief and straight on to recovery. She said it was never too late to fix the relationship with her children but she had to be alive to do it. Messing with those drugs she may not live long enough. Then Mercedes said although she understood why I flipped and blacked out on Shatease, she wishes I would have handled it a different way by waiting until after she had the baby. She also said she hoped I flipped on Griff the same way and that Mike did have a point when he said that I was the only one who thought it was a relationship with Griff. Mercedes reiterated Griff didn't belong to me and I knew what it was hitting for because he never made a secret of Nakisha. In fact he always

[116]

claimed her but he never claimed me. She said she didn't want to hurt my feelings but reminded me of him and Kiki at the party and how he looked at me and shrugged as if to say so what?

I held up my hands then for her to cease the topic of conversation. I knew if Mercedes kept talking, I would never go through with my end of tonight's scheme. If not for nothing else, I had to go through with it for Mike and the memory of my homey Beemie, who knocked out grown men for me.

As far as I knew Mike always kept it one hundred with me. He needed me just as much as Griff did. I reached in my food bag and pulled out my lukewarm hamburger. Mercedes asked me if I wanted her to nuke it in the microwave. I told her no that it would just make it kind of gooey to chew. I took a big bite and Mercedes came over and rubbed my hair. She told me to change my hairstyle. Maybe rock a short pixy cut, boost a new outfit and go out for a little mini girls' night out. She said although I was young, I didn't really look it when my make-up was done and I should be able to get into the low budget bar with her to have a drink. I told her I was leaving pretty soon and didn't know if I would be back any time soon or if I would return at all.

I was feeling some type of way about living in New York City and felt it was time to spread my wings. She looked at me inquisitively but didn't say anything.

She just shook her head up and down as if to say she hears me. I ate and droned on and on until I noticed I had ten minutes to get to the Management Office on 143rd street.

I asked Mercedes for her spare key so I wouldn't disturb her on my way back in. She looked hesitant but saw me getting antsy and then scurried over to her closet, reached up on the top shelf and grabbed the key.

"Bingo," she stated, then scooted over to give it to me, "I know I am not your mother, please just not too late while on my watch. I have a tendency to worry."

I told her that I understood and I would try my best to finish my business and get back to the house. I asked her if she needed me to bring her anything from the house on her way back in. She said just bring a gallon of water. She hated to drink tap water.

Mercedes crazy ass told me she think the government puts something in the water because all the little niggas around here started to dress weird and crazy; like they were gay or something. She started cracking up telling me about Ms. Sylvia's grandson Matt who was in the hallway popping gum with skinny jeans on snapping his fingers talking about 'Ooh girl, no he didn't'. She said when she got closer he was talking about how the man farted in his face and his balls were stink. She said she almost had a heart attack and how things weren't like that when she was younger.

She also think he is the first openly gay man or teen rather she ever really knew personally. She said it took all her might not to ask him why the fuck he wants somebody balls in his mouth but then decided against it because it's a new day and age and as long as her son or grandson was straight it didn't affect her one way or another who had a dick in their mouth or who balls were hitting the back of whose throat. As long as they didn't push that shit on her she was good. She cracked up laughing again imitating Matt. As for me, I didn't really see anything funny. Maybe because I was still hurting I didn't feel the need to belittle anyone for their choices. I politely excused myself by saying I would catch her later. I kissed her on the cheek and walked so fast people thought I was the crack head on the mission.

Chapter 8

Making it to the management office in ten minutes flat, Fuquan was already standing around waiting for me. He grabbed me by the arm and told me it was a change in plans. The original guise of paying their rent wouldn't work because Griff was adamant on doing it at night time. He also told me that he told Sassy it was on some type of beef tip using me as the bait. He said it might require that I knuckle up and fight her. Any other time I would have been on my bully shit. However, I wasn't feeling this new plan at all. Not one to make my squad become disappointed in me because I couldn't handle their directives, started cracking my knuckles and snaking my neck then said, "Aight, I am with it."

We walked to stand behind Mott Haven Projects, close to the church on the block. Fuquan had on a hoodie since it was a little breezy and I had on a light blue sleeveless shirt and some ripped up acid wash jeans. Shivering, I asked him what was taking Sassy so long and told him I was getting cold. He wrapped his arms around me. He told me not to worry Sassy should be walking up on the scene in a minute. After standing in that embrace, rocking back and forth with each other for what seemed like five minutes, Sassy walked up with a crew of girls talking loud and pointing at me. Not caught off guard but totally in a state of disbelief it finally hit me. I also silently wondered if the main target was her brother why did he tell her I was the one with beef. How was that going to get her brother William in the position to be the victim? As I went to throw up my dick beaters, I heard screeching of the tires. I was lost temporarily until I heard the first round go off. Fuquan grabbed me on some old 'Matrix' type grip and we spun and fell in between two parked cars. The rounds hitting Sassy propelled her body forward and she fell with a thud. I heard what sounded like a grunt and noticed she was face down on the concrete. Her eyes were open staring at us and blood was seeping from each wound. The girls she was with started screaming and Fuquan jumped up, brushed his clothes off and then snatched me by the back of my shirt, "Come on. We have to go."

He dragged me part way back towards his building and then let me go and told me to slow down my pace and walk naturally. He informed me the rest of the crew should be coming soon. I was then reminded by him to get rid of the deadly weapon. He told me Griff said he would catch up with me about four in the morning and just be prepared to leave for the o.t. trip.

I was feeling overwhelmed to say the least. I thought I would have a couple days to at least get prepared for another criminal activity. I bit my lip hard and tasted blood. I figured I must have re-opened my wound. Upon hearing me say ow, Fuquan grabbed my face by the chin and asked me what happened. Trying to keep my strong resolve, I told him nothing much just a disagreement with ma dukes that went a little too far.

He told me for what it's worth he has been in the projects long enough to know crackheads can do some fucked up shit but remember she is the only parent I have so for the sake of my siblings to deal with her a little more tenderly. I thought he must have bumped his head when we hit the dirt. Since when did this thug care about family events or affairs of the heart? He asked me if that is why I was so lost in space thinking about my mother. Not wanting to seem like a complete fool or asshole, I told him that was exactly it. I didn't want to tell him that Griff was the main one in my mind frame taking up space. He came to put his arms around me again and Griff walked up on the scene as if on cue.

Fuquan hesitated to complete his already started action and dropped his hand to his side. Griff reached out and gave him a man hug and told him payment would be handed out in the morning. He told Fuquan he appreciated him looking out on the retaliation move for his family. Until we arrived back from out of town to watch his back against William and the rest of the Rough Houser's. Griff also told him, he was going to personally take care of William but he wanted him to stew and wallow in grief and guilt like he was doing himself over Beemie. I stood to the side biting my nail to the nub. This is who I didn't want to see right now as the feelings were still raw. I peeped Donnie snidely walking up on Griff's blindside and then he asked could he speak with him for a moment. He startled Griff. However, Griff excused himself to go and talk with Donnie. While his back was turn Fuquan hugged me a little tightly. He told me he was going on home and to be safe out in these Bronx streets. He quickly but tenderly kissed me on the side of my face and I took my arm which was wrapped around his body and gave his back a pat. I told him I got him and not to worry I was in good hands.

He started laughing, "Yea, I bet."

Fuquan then started to walk backwards and pointed at us individually while yelling, "Ayo, G-money, I'mma holler at you in the morning. Peace Donnie D. Later!"

Fuquan quickly turned around and put a little more pep in his step, he threw his hoodie back on his head and started singing 'However, do you want me? However, do you need me?' by Soul to Soul, another one of my mother's jams.

I started shaking my leg again and wishing Griff would come on. I realized by this time him and Donnie were in each other's face and arguing about money. Donnie was telling Griff there wasn't anything in this life free and he wanted payment for his services.

"Ayo Donnie, go ahead with all that man," he started saying while shaking his head, "Payment is disbursed to all the players at the same time home boy and not a minute before that. You understand me? Now keep it moving before you don't get shit."

Griff turned around to walk back towards me and Donnie snuck him with a sucker punch. Griff was taken by surprise but he didn't fall. He was rattled but didn't drop. He swung around and Donnie rushed him like they were playing tackle football. Part of me wanted to see Griff get his ass kicked. He was so damn disrespectful and uncaring when it came to my feelings. I thought, why I should care about if he gets knocked around at all. It served him right for his antagonizing, womanizing ways.

Donnie and Griff fell into a SUV that was double parked and 'got it shaking' as my cousins from Mt. Vernon always said. It was pretty good but Donnie did seem to be a little more in command of the fight. All in all I say Donnie was winning and Griff was a good contender. Watching and moving with each blow that was doled out I gasped when Donnie did some old sweeper move and knocked Griff's feet from under him. He fell on his back hard and his head bounced off the concrete. That was it Griff was done.

Donnie used nothing but feet and was kicking the hell out of Griff. Feeling bad I looked for a weapon and saw an old broomstick someone had discarded. I grabbed it and said, "Back off Donnie. That's enough. Leave him be."

Donnie was too far gone. He wasn't paying any attention to me. I seriously doubt that he heard me. After he realized Griff was done he started digging in his pockets. I snapped out of my daze and realized no matter what I said Donnie wasn't going to cease his assault so I started hitting him with the broom but he still didn't budge.

Donnie then started searching Griff's pockets. He kept finding money in various places on Griff's body and saying, "Jackpot!" or "Score".

Griff was mumbling something so I took the broom and reeled back then brought it down on Donnie's head as hard as I could. It nudged him forward. He held out his hand to catch himself from falling. He looked back at me and snarled, having nothing to gain but everything to lose if he got off that concrete, raised the broom again and clunked it over his head. I did this about three more times until he fell flat on his face. I scrambled to help Griff off the floor thinking to myself all the time I still loved him. I wrapped his arm around my neck and grabbed him by the waist and struggled to lift him up. Once on his two feet we moved as fast as his wounded body would let us. He was coughing slightly hard and I awkwardly patted his back.

"You alright Griffin Aloysius Montgomery" I asked him using his full given name. He rubbed the back of his head and started chuckling. I guess it was to keep away the embarrassment of getting his ass kicked in front of a girl who admired him. Secretly underneath the laugh, I felt his pain. We made it to the building and called Mike to assist us. He came down to the lobby as fast as he could and grabbed Griff arm from around me.

"I got you playboy. Everything's going to be cool." Mike said overly concerned, "When we get in the door speak in low tones, big mama just went to bed. I don't need her getting up and worrying about anything."

"Alright, we hear you," I said a little annoyed. I wanted to just make sure Griff was alright without all the extra shenanigans. I felt Marie would be alright with a little noise in her life. It was not like we was having a wild ass party. Mike seemed to slow down a little and looked at me as if to say, 'Do we have a problem.' I looked at him and cut my eyes and said, "Damn, he might be bleeding internally."

This was an attempt to take the heat of Mike's gaze off of me and put it back where it belonged and that was our mutual homeboy. We bumped awkwardly on the elevator as we all tried to rush in at the same time,

Mike pressed his floor. Griff kept coughing and I stood in the back of them with my leg shaking violently. Mike kept looking at me and cutting his eyes. I really didn't think my attitude in saying we heard him warranted those looks. We made it to Mike's door and he went in first and left us in the hall. He wanted to make sure Marie was still in the bed where he left her. After five minutes he came and helped Griff to the futon. He told me to stay in the hall for a moment.

Becoming nervous because I didn't know what laid in store for me. I mean they told me one plan about killing William and wound up killing the sister. Maybe just maybe they were going to kill me too. My leg went to twitching again and I almost fainted thinking about what could have been my fate. It seemed eerily quiet and the wait was long. Then I heard Mike coming back towards the front door. In his hand was a gun that looked a lot like the one my Uncle Mack gave Griff for his retaliation against William. I started sweating profusely and my knees started to buckle.

"Mike, wait," I started but he thrust the gun in my hand and banged it against my chest.

"Here, take this down to the bridge leading to the FDR and dispose of it. Make sure you closer to the Manhattan side and dingo," he paused.

"Yes, I said becoming impatient, "What the hell is it?"

"Watch your tone first of all. Second of all use common sense and wipe all fingerprints off; third of all, good looking on bringing him here to my house. You do have some street sense and loyalty. Fourth of all, I need you back here a.s.a.p. after you dispose of that. I think his ribs might be bruised or broke. You are going to have to sit with him in Lincoln Hospital Emergency Room. When the doctor ask what happened, say you two were on a double date at the theater on 161st street and some locals came in acting rowdy. Words were exchanged and Griff got the brakes and the soul beat out of his body. Do you think you can handle all that?"

"Does butter taste good on toast?" I said laughing. Mike laughed as well and then closed the door saying, "Aight, go handle that."

I went to do Mike's bidding and prepared myself to sit in this most likely crowded ass emergency room. Lord knows I couldn't handle it. I used to go with my mother when one of my siblings were struck by an asthma attack. Thank God Asthma skipped me but the other three received SSI checks since theirs were so bad. Just then I remembered I never got to ask my mother what she did with Junior's checks. The realization that she got checks for the other children and we still lived like we was dead poor with no income sickened me. I wished I was older to take my younger siblings. My mother thought I was a joke but I would have the last laugh.

Having the gun tucked on my waist, I prayed no one would mess with me. I swear carrying heavy artillery made me feel invincible. That is why I was so quick to pull the trigger on the Rough Houser after Beemie's funeral. It just felt so right.

I threw the murder weapon into the East River and made treks back to the Bronx. I walked briskly because Mike called to inform me something was seriously wrong with Griffin. I told him if that was the case call for the ambulance and send him ahead of me. Instead of coming back to the building I would just head over to Lincoln. He said he spotted blood in Griffin's spit and it was a mucus type texture. Despite these new circumstances Griff didn't want to go into the emergency room because he had to leave in about two hours for this trip. Mike told me Griff was instructing me to hurry up even faster because he just wanted to board the train to get to Texas as soon as possible.

Remembering my Uncle Mack had a doctor on his payroll for instances like this, I walked a little more quickly. Upon getting to Mike's apartment door, I heard muffled voices. From what I could make out it was Nakisha and she was arguing with Griff. Not knowing exactly how to feel, I pressed my ear up to the actual door and continued listening.

"Why I have to get a call from my cousin telling me Griff was outside getting stomped on. He was mercilessly beat all in the street and no one calls me?" Nakisha was ranting and raving.

"Yo, if you don't hold your voice down, I am going to put you out. My Grandmother is sleeping. Show some respect." Mike countered her loud mouth antics with some bass in his last statement. I am not sure of the look on her face, if her mouth dropped open or not but the silence was golden. After a few seconds I heard Griff have another coughing attack. I raised my hand to knock on the door but paused for a moment to stop and think if I really felt like going through anymore confrontations. All in the course of a night, I managed to fight my mother, best friend, watch a young girl get murdered and saved the man I hated to be in love with from getting his soul stomped out of him. The hesitation however ended as soon as it began. I wanted this bitch Nakisha to know I wasn't going anywhere no matter what Griff told her. I brought my hand down and knocked loud and rapidly.

"God dam it", was all I heard Mike say, "Now what is it and who the fuck could this be?"

Mike was irritated and I didn't blame him. From what I could tell he didn't have a steady girlfriend so why Griff's girlfriend should be bothering him in his own house. She was yelling and making a scene while his grandmother was resting.

He flung open the door and rolled his eyes when he noticed it was me. Then he replied, "I would tell you to wait outside but this business is important. You two be very civilized and I won't have to put my wife beaters on anybody."

I laughed when Mike said this; he simply meant he didn't want to have to put his hands on me or Nakisha. I walked in and rolled my eyes at Nakisha. She simply sucked her teeth and said under her breath, "Lord, not this young, dumb bitch."

"Aye, watch your mouth. Better yet tell me how my pussy is tasting since your man be sucking all on my clit!" I shouted. I really didn't have to respect this hoe Nakisha. I would have played nice if she had left the bitch word out of her mouth when seeing me. I didn't understand how a woman lost a fight to someone and still talked shit. You'd think she'd eat humble pie every time she seen me.

However, I was slowly starting to realize in the dealings with my mother and Shatease that some people were gluttons for punishment. I almost cried again when the realization hit me for a second time that my god-daughter's mother and best friend was a crack addict. At fifteen she was pregnant and had a two year old child. From the information I was able to grasp she doesn't know who the father of the second child is and could even be from the man I am involved with. To add insult to injury she was a crack addict when I thought she didn't even do hard drugs. Now in the dealings I had with these two who were the epitome of 'These hoes ain't loyal' chicks made me think Nakisha would be willing to remain humble? I took a couple of steps toward her and watched her cringe then try and play it off. I started laughing as I figured I could use Nakisha face as a punching bag to relieve some of the frustrations from the revelations of today's events. She started huffing and puffing but I wasn't fazed by this bitch.

I looked at Mike and asked him did he think I could use the bathroom. He said yes. I went in the compact but neat bathroom with the blue shark shower curtains and pulled out my cell phone. Dialing my Uncle Mack's number, I started humming Soul to Soul, like I heard Fuquan singing. A smile crept on my face as the smooth jazz tunes my uncle chose for his ring tone started playing in my ear. After the fifth ring, the call was sent to voicemail. I left a message telling my uncle I was going to call right back and please pick up the phone next time it rang. I hopped about from one foot to the other not believing my life and this mess then was startled as my uncle called me back.

"Hey Unc what's it hitting for" I asked in my usual greeting to him. I listened intently as he asked me if everything was okay because he spoke to my mother. He wanted to know where I was going to be because he was going to send for me and allow me to stay with him until things blew over. He also told me that even though it was unfair of him to ask me this would I mind making up with my mother for the sake of my younger siblings? He just didn't want his brother's children winding up in the system and without a responsible person in the home to ensure they took their baths and ate, his fear might just materialize. I told him he didn't have to think twice about asking me. Those were my siblings and I had the same fear. I found my bargaining chip and said I wouldn't hesitate to go back if I had one wish that he could make come true. Without hesitation, my Uncle Mack said, "Sure baby girl what is it?"

I set him up by telling him all about today's events minus the real reason for the fight with Shatease. I just said it was because her baby Yannie had a crack pipe in her hand. I could tell my uncle listened with bated breath, then I hit him with what the real favor was. I told him that Griff had been harmed in a street fight and I was able to come to his defense. I mentioned Griff didn't want to let him down so I wanted to ride shotgun on his trip to Texas. I also told him that Griff was coughing up blood and if he could get his doctor friend to pay a visit to him before we started traveling. My uncle was so quiet I just knew he was going to shoot my ideas down. However, he said it would all be fine and he would meet us in Dallas instead of Houston as originally planned. My uncle said to give him Mike's address and he would send the doctor on his way a.s.a.p.

Flying out the bathroom to tell the guys my good news and to score some brownie points over Nakisha, I was once again faced with reality. Lo and behold, Nakisha was sitting on the sofa with Griff, his arm was draped around her shoulder. She was gazing up into his face with a smile so damn bright I wanted to knock the living shit out of her. I wanted to hit her so hard she flew through the wormhole into another existence.

Since it was already four o'clock in the morning, I broke up the little love fest and told everyone that I was leaving. I also informed the trio my Uncle Mack was sending a doctor over to check Griffin out so we could get ready for our departure to Texas but I wouldn't be ready until the morning. Mike looked at me with the side eye and shook his head like, "Damn, this chick is a mess."

Nakisha at first didn't think she heard me correctly and asked me for clarity. I didn't hesitate to take this chance to bring her up to speed.

"Griffin, kindly tell your chicken head who is pulling the strings on this venture, who is riding shotgun and who you asked to get ready to carry your children?"

Okay, I was clowning and he really didn't ask me to have his babies but I wanted to play with her emotions any way I could. Mike spit out the juice he was drinking and had to stop himself from yelling at me, "Alright little Ms. It's time for you to get to stepping."

Griffin looked at me all bugged eye and told Nakisha I was just playing about the babies but it was my hook up that landed him this gun smuggling opportunity. She looked at me long and hard then stated, "Well," all the while rubbing Griff's chest up and down, "I think I could grab a couple of days off from work. I can log on from anywhere to turn my school assignments in so that shouldn't be too much of an issue."

Mike giggled and looked at me like, 'Oops, what are you going to say now?'

Griff looked uncomfortable and also seemed to be at a loss for words. I, however, wasn't. "Oh, I am sorry Nastinksta, umm that is your name correct?"

She huffed at the mispronunciation of her name and I continued, "Given our history, meaning yours and mine, you are not allowed to accompany us. See, I would hate to get all the way to Virginia and have to wind up kicking your ass and leaving you on the side of the road. If you insist on coming, I will call my Uncle and tell him to cancel Griff's role in the plan and I would then nominate to him another one of his soldiers. Griff would then lose out on one hundred and fifty big ones. Now if you decide your man, whom is going to need the majority of that skrilla to help you all in whatever adventures you two be going on, should be the one to get that money you would sit your old wanna be up my ass down. Really, let this be a lesson to you that sometimes the help becomes the savior and the next time you want to spit in a bitch's face make sure you can match their long paper or connections for that matter."

I eyed her very carefully. I took note of the different emotions registering on her face. I couldn't exactly call what decision she came to but she sat back and whispered to Griff, "Let this be the only time that young chick get to call any shots over me. I don't like it. I mean ever since she has supposedly been your 'soldier/worker' our relationship has seem to be going downhill. Pretty soon you are going to have to make a decision as to her or me."

I smirked listening to her, then wrenched the knife already in her heart to let her know whose fault it really was that she couldn't be a part of our team, "Or maybe you should tell yourself to make sure you don't spit on anymore bosses. I obviously call the shots on this business venture so with that being said I am going to holler at you Griffin in about four hours after I get some sleep and you get checked out by my Uncle's doctor,"

I got up and started heading to the door, stopped, turned around and stated, "Oh, and if I hear that bitch in the background I still will call my Uncle Mack with a new change of plans,"

Taking cue from Fuquan I started pointing at them and said, "Ayo, catch you all later!"

Once outside and out of the trio's earshot, I started laughing to myself. I may have been a fool but this chick was a straight up dummy. How did she think her rank pussy could make a young dealer from the projects faithful to her? I know for a fact I wasn't the only girl she caught him with. I am certain there were more than I even knew about.

Every chance I get I planned on making her ass miserable the same way I was when I saw them go out on their outings together, holding hands or snuggled up like a happy little couple.

I started walking back towards Millbrook. My plan was to get to Mercedes house as fast as possible. I knew she probably was sick with worry about me. I could honestly say even though she had her problems she loved me and Shatease whole heartedly. I put a little pep in my step due to the brisk air. I turned around because I heard someone calling my name. Damn, it was Fuquan. I really wanted to get some rest and didn't have time for the ritual of hugging up and bullshitting. I told him as much and he said he would walk me to Millbrook but he had some beef with certain people over there. I told him after all the excitement we had for the night his best bet was to play the house until things cooled off. He asked me to play the house with him. I hesitated and thought what could it hurt. I would call Mercedes but she didn't have minutes on her phone. She had to figure I wouldn't be coming back tonight and if something was truly wrong one of my home girls would have knocked on her door.

Giving in, I told Fuquan, I could only stay for around three and a half hours. I told him Griff and I were motivating to the dirty south to go make this paper. He said he didn't think Texas was the dirty south but okay and he wanted to spend more time with me now than ever in case I caught a case or something. Then he started laughing when I punched him in his arm.

"Hey, the fuck wrong with you? Why would you jinx me like that?" I asked him, hoping he was only playing around. He put me in a playful headlock and we went into the liquor store. He got three small nips of no named vodka and then went to the bodega to get some backwoods cigar papers. I scrunched up my face at this selection and he said he's buying so it's his choice what we use to smoke our weed in. I just threw my hands up as if to say you got it and played the background as he chose the munchies as well. We arrived at Fuquan's house where we smoked and drank for a while. We did our usual ritual of foreplay and no sex. Things did get heavy but I was on the last day of my period and in true gangster fashion Fuquan said, "I don't run red lights."

I smiled thinking to myself you had to be leery of
motherfuckers that do. I don't know too much about
HIV/AIDS but from what I gathered it was blood to
blood contact or any bodily fluids for that matter. I
didn't want to be sick at a young age so it was
foreplay and oral sex mostly for now. Fuquan had
baby daddy potential but I was too stuck on Griff to
put it into motion.

Chapter 9

Fuquan and I drifted off into a deep sleep intertwined in each other's arms. My shirt and bra was off but my panties was still on. He was butt naked with his long, thick meat slung over on the side of his leg. I heard my phone in the distance of my dreams going off. I couldn't pull myself through the haze to answer it. In the distance of my dreams was my King Shaleeq. He was standing in the same clothes he was murdered in. He looked at me and asked me if I was happy? When I realized he wasn't talking to me but Shatease, I began to cry. Why I thought even in my dreams no one seemed to love me. I started to bawl out to him and ask him, "Daddy, it's me, your baby girl Koi-Koi. Don't you recognize me?"

My king seem to look right past me and continue talking to Shatease, "Tell Bianca at one time she meant the world to me."

I started bugging in my dreams and ran to hit Shatease but an invisible wall stopped me. I turned and looked at my dad, who was once my life and I thought I was his and asked him, "Daddy, don't you love me?"

As I looked steadily into my father's eyes all I saw was fire. His mouth opened, "Koi-Koi, the name sounds familiar but unless you are kin to my wife Angela I think you have got the wrong man. I am not your pappy."

Bewildered by his statement and wondering why and how he knew or acknowledged Shatease and her mother Bianca and not me his own child. How could he call me kin to his wife but not his love bug or princess Koi-Koi like he used to. Upon realizing his eyes caught ablaze, I woke up in a sweat filled puddle. I grabbed my shirt and held it up to my chest when I realized there was a girl who looked like a gorilla staring at me. "Umm, may I help you?" I asked bothered. She looked at me, rolled her eyes and started throwing things at Fuquan.

"Nigga, get the fuck up. You got me twisted if you think you gone just play me with these little itty bitty bitches." She was whooping, hollering and flinging things at us. I told her to chill before I fucked her shit up. She laughed at me. I started getting up off the bed and trying to put my shirt over my head at the same time. I was so petite compared to this bitch but I didn't let size fool or scare me and obviously she did. I guess she didn't know I had the anger that could fill a football stadium and I was willing to take it out on her as I did Shatease earlier.

I may have had a questionable fight with my mother earlier but in no means was this linebacker going get away with it and not get some bruising to show her she had a run in with a Boss. I was doing the one step dance trying not to fall as I put on my pants. The bitch kept talking and throwing things so I was going to beat the brakes off the beast. Fuquan was sitting up in a daze, trying to grasp the serious situation at hand. It must have hit him because he jumped off the bed and started trying to hold me back and get at her at the same time.

"What the fuck Mere? I already told you it was over? Who the fuck let you in here?" he said unapologetically.

"Fuck you mean? You told me what Fu? Last time we spoke you was saying how good it was and you couldn't wait to spend time with me and Merequan. I don't think I misunderstood you, so, fuck you talking about you told me it was over?"

She sounded hurt and dejected and I figured I better let them handle their family squabble. Far be it from me to break up anyone's home if they had children. All others were fair game though.

I finished dressing and putting on my footwear while keeping an eagle eye on his baby mother. I know if she was anything like me she would just go on and attack my little ass. I didn't play with anyone's emotions when hurt and I doubt she would play with mine as well.

I told Fuquan, I would let him handle his family squabble because I had business to attend to. I reached up and wrapped my arm around his neck and he bent down to kiss me. After a quick but sensual kiss on the lips I looked on at Shamere, his baby mother as I walked out his door. When I got to the brightly yellow painted living room there were some kids giggling who tried to straighten up when they noticed I was in the room. After giving them the sternest look I could muster I shook my head and mumbled, "Children these days."

Realizing, I forgot my phone in Fuquan's room made an about face to go retrieve it. When I got to the door, I heard her crying asking him not to hit her anymore. I took a deep breath and went in the room. He paused his swing in midair and asked me what the fuck I was staring at? Not knowing what to say I told him my purpose for returning. I grabbed my phone and as I raced out the door, I told him she had learned her lesson; he should let her go. He shrugged his shoulders and said, "Word right?" then he punched the shit out of her.

She fell to the floor, wrenching and moaning and I just walked out the door saying 'damn, better her than me'.

Realizing that it was almost afternoon I wondered if Griff left me or what was the status of his health according to the doctor my Uncle Mack sent to assist him.

I checked my phone as I quickened my step and realized Griff and Mike left about twenty messages. Some messages were the usual 'where you at?', 'You need to hurry the fuck up' and some messages were very angry and violent saying how I was fucking up his money and he was going to fuck me up if I didn't call him in the next few minutes. One message even went as far to say, 'how the fuck are you going to let your feelings for my wifey get in the way of this major paper? I thought you were smarter than that? You knew what it was before I ever had any dealings with you. I suggest you get your mind right and call me within the next few hours the train is set to leave at three.' I checked my watch and it was one thirty in the afternoon.

I didn't really have any clothes to take and thought about my blank prescription papers. I figured they would be safe at Mercedes house until I returned.

My uncle was sending Griff and me to Texas with about six hundred grand besides Griff's fee. He was going to meet us in Dallas but felt it was important in case we had to pay our way out of some jams. He told us the money was mainly to stay at the best tourist hotel and visit a few attractions until he met up with us. In him doing that I didn't even have a care in the world or have to worry about clothes since he also told Griff to give me twenty five grand out of the money so I can go on a shopping spree. I thought to myself that all this time I thought my Uncle Mack was a low budget hustler and he was sitting on stacks. I was amazed and thought now more than ever I wanted to take over his business. If I was able to keep it running smoothly like him then my siblings and I could be straight. I might just look out for Angela, my mother as well. However, doing anything for her was still up in the air.

My new worry though was to get a message to Mercedes and tell her I should be back in two weeks tops and to reserve my spot on the sofa. I looked across the street and realized the phone store was open. I ran in and paid some minutes on her wireless. I then dialed her number. She answered around the third time I called her. She said she was surprised that her phone would ring. She really was overjoyed and kept thanking me and told me to be safe on my journey. I told her I would and then hung up. I jumped on the elevator and decided I wouldn't call Mike and Griff but just knock on the door.

As soon as I knocked I heard Griff very distinctly say 'It better be Koi or I am fucking her up when I see her'.

I giggled at him. He was always so antsy and threatening to fuck someone up when he couldn't get his way but after I saw Donnie put the beats to him I was hardly scared. I sashayed my ass on in the middle of the living room and said, "Yea, whatever. Save that shit for someone who is scared to throw you the deuces. Now what the fuck is up and why are you sweating me?"

He looked at me with daggers in his eyes and replied, "Yo, Shorty don't fuck with me. You fucking with my paper. You were supposed to be here hours ago and no one seen your little ass. I mean fuck was you doing that is more important than making this green paper?"

"Oh, I thought you were busy with your wifey. Also for your information, I could give two fucks about you and her relationship. You been doing you and now I am doing me. Ya feel me?"

I rolled my eyes and clapped my hands for emphasis to help him realize I was serious.

"Yo, check this here. I'm not playing with your little ass. I suggest you change your tone and get your priorities straight before I have to get it shaking in these streets."

I giggled to myself, how convenient it all is in his world. I am supposed to sit back while he run with every chick there is and when the time arises that I want to move on he decides to get it shaking.

I rolled my eyes and snaked my neck again and said, "Yea, whatever, nigga!"

Mike closely watched the interaction and shook his head. He piped in and said, "Glad, I am single and everyone knows it. So there are no misconceptions when one bitch bucks up on the other. They all know the chosen one for the night is the one I am with and the other waits her turn."

We all laughed for a moment over Mike's self-proclaimed player status.

Changing the subject, I turned back to Griff and said, "I am here now homey, what it hitting for? We leaving or what, it's two fifteen in the afternoon. Call the cab to take us to Penn station. I am ready to get the ball rolling. I feel like we have been plotting forever. You need this dough and I need to see more of this beautiful country."

He told Mike to call us a cab and pass his duffle bag. He reached into the bag and took out a crisp red, round collared tee shirt. He took off the dingy black one he had on. That is when I noticed his chest and mid-section was taped up in white bandages. I asked him if the doctor did the tape job on him and if so what was the outcome of his exam?

Griff informed me that one or two of his ribs were broken and the tape sort of acted as a brace for them. He said there was no real procedure but to deal with the pain as his ribs healed on their own. He explained the doctor gave him some top of the line pain killers. Griff further explained since he hated prescription pills for the fact he might get addicted, he will only take a few when the pain was excruciating. He said the rest he would sell when he returned from Texas.

I watched as he didn't even use a wash rag to wipe under his arms but just threw some degree deodorant on.

He looked at me and said, "What you never seen a dude freshen up before?"

I asked him, "Where's the soap and water, homie?"

Mike fell out laughing and said he could see why we had dealings with each other. We were perfect together like salt and vinegar on a hero or something to that effect.

The cab driver called when he was downstairs and Mike helped Griffin up off the futon.

Mike's Grandmother Marie came in the living room and gave Griff her best wishes. She really didn't know what was going on but knew he was going out of town. He hobbled over to her and kissed her gingerly on the cheek and told her he would be careful. She then turned and looked and me with a

[149]

knowingly look and asked me, "When's the last time you seen Angela?"

I told her it had been about a day or so as we had a disagreement. Not fully believing me she asked me my age, "So, ummm you are like sixteen, seventeen? I guess that is why the system didn't take you. I just hope they keep the children together. If I had more room I would damn sure take you all even the autistic teen. God says to help others and I will. If they are not able to be placed together I can probably find someone from the church to assist and take them all. You just let me know honey."

I was floored and flabbergasted. I don't think I had been gone two full days yet for the children to be gone. I questioned Mike's grandmother further, "Ma'am, I am sorry. I am not understanding what you are saying. Are you referring to my family, Angela Bettenfield and the MacDougal children?"

"Yes, I am honey. The cops swooped in early to mid-morning today. It seemed she got caught steering and they slapped the cuffs on her. When she resisted and tried to appeal to the officers by saying her children were upstairs and she needed to get back to them, they asked the children's ages and went to investigate and found them. The reports I overheard from the neighbors were that the kids were disheveled and the place was a mess.

They asked the children when were the last time they had eaten anything. They said yesterday because their mother cashed in the stamps and their older sister had run away because mommy beat her. That is you right, the older sister? I thought you were a little younger?"

My heart was broken as I wondered the same thing Marie did. Were they able to keep the children together in the same home? I figured I better call my Uncle Mack from inside the cab and tell him his worst fear had materialized.

I moved in and hugged Marie and thanked her for informing me of the latest update on my family. I told her I didn't know if we needed the church member's assistance yet as I had one family member who cared and might be able to assist. She just put her arm back around me and patted my back and said, "Anytime, dear, anytime."

Mike told us to break up the moment as the cab was waiting and we only had a limited time to get to the station. Griff hobbled as fast as he could behind us to the elevator. I was so engrossed in my thoughts on how to tell my Uncle Mack the latest development on the MacDougal kids that I never saw Milk and Bam come from out the exit with guns drawn.

They knocked me over the head and went to blasting at Griff and Mike. I don't know how Griff and Mike managed to pull their weapons as well. I crawled up in a fetal position and jumped each time I heard a round fired. Then I heard Bam screaming, "Aw shit, Milk you hit homey,"

As Milk fell back against the exit door, it opened and Donnie stepped through. I scrambled back, damn near spider walking trying to get to Mike grandmother's apartment. Mike had rounded a corner mad fast. I swear he was an expert marksmen because once every couple of seconds he would peep out from behind the wall and hit Milk or Bam with a round while Griff was laid on the floor with one eye open and the other closed he let off the fatal round into Milk's head which caused him to fall back and Bam to scream.

I placed my hand behind me as I backed up and finally hit Mike's apartment door and started banging. I heard Marie screaming, "Mike, Mike, Oh my God is that you?" and the sound of feet shuffling.

I started screaming and banging for her to open the door as I saw Bam start walking in my direction, "Marie, it's me Koi, Angela's daughter. Please, please open the door ma'am."

I heard one lock unturned then I heard Mike scream out, "Mama, don't you open that shit."

I don't know what I really expected but it damn sure wasn't to hear him say that. While I know I think I am grown the realization suddenly hit me that I was only a child playing in a grown person's world. I begged God a million different ways as I saw Bam

[152]

raise the gun after me to help me out of this jam. I bargained with God that if he allowed me to live past this moment, I wouldn't run the streets any longer and would concentrate on bettering myself. I guess God must have known I was probably lying because Bam pulled the trigger and it slammed into my shoulder. The left side of my body banged into the door. I screamed, "Oh God, Bam, why? Oh why me?"

He started cocking back the hammer again and said something that resonated with Mike, Griff and myself, "Don't you know Rough Houser's don't fall we come a million strong?"

"Huh," was all I managed before the next shot went off and hit me in my knee. I moved the hand that was untouched and grabbed my leg and then I heard two shots in succession. Bam's head split open like a machete slicing a watermelon and Griff screamed, "Yes, fucking traitor. You are an ass; a pussy ass nigga's bitch. Donnie, what you thinking yawl niggas turn coats on the team Fam? Yawl want to see how Mike and the Griff man play with Fuck boys? Bring your ass out that exit homeboy right now!"

Mike peered from around the corner and asked Griff if he was alright? Griff nodded and told him he was in good condition. Mike looked for me and called out to me to see if I was okay.

"Mike, I'm hit! I'm hit!" I screamed wanting him to make it all better. He told me to calm down and the main thing would be to maintain my composure to avoid going into shock. He said that would be the last thing we needed at the moment. I started breathing heavy and feeling a little cold and queasy.

"Mike, I think I am dying. I feel too cold. I read about this before."

I could hear his grandmother Marie screaming, "Mike baby I can't let that baby die like that in the hallway. I am opening up this door."

"Granny don't you open that damn door. She's hit and it don't make sense for the two of you to wind up in no one's hospital. I am not playing about this shit," he yelled at his grandmother and I was starting to fade in and out of consciousness.

"Don't you sass me young man. I am a God fearing Christian woman and I don't fear no man nor bullet and that baby is not going to die in this hallway not after I helped take care of her father Shaleeq."

I could hear the door knob turning after numerous clicks. The door swung open and somehow Marie managed to grab me in her apartment. She slammed the door back after peeking her head out the door. She yelled for Mike and Griff to come on until she could get the police up to the apartment. Mike was adamant that he wasn't going in the apartment. In his mind he listed all the reasons he should stand his ground in the hallway. The main reason was he needed to be able to defend his grandmother's house against all attacks and couldn't see if he was behind the metal door instead of in front of it. He felt like he would die in that hallway making sure no harm came to his grandmother. She put her own life on hold to take him in and raise him and her last act of kindness or heroism, in his eyes, was casting fear for losing her life to the side and opening up the door to drag Koi inside out of harm of any more bullets. He looked at Griffin whom he didn't hear from in a while and he seemed to look so peaceful. Mike instantly felt tears spring to his eyes as he came to the realization that Griffin was more than likely dead. He saw at least two bullet holes in his lower chest cavity area and blood seeping from them.

Mike saw a movement and then a flash. He jumped back to his corner and breathed quick and steadily. He counted to three and then popped his head out to peek. He saw Donnie standing over Griff with his gun aimed for his head and then he stated rather harshly, "Don't you wish now you would have gave me my money when I asked for it playa?"

Then he laughed and took the safety off. Mike wasted no time and fired a lethal headshot. He watched as Donnie's head flew back from the impact of the bullet. Mike then blew his gun's barrel and screamed, "Bull's eye."

He tucked the gun in his pants and heard the cops' radio on the elevator. "Oh shit," he thought, I better get the fuck out of here. He maneuvered around the dead bodies and ran into the stair case exit. He ran up two flights to one of his good friend's house. He knocked rapidly on the door and waited impatiently. It took about five minutes for a response and as he heard the cops' radio in the staircase exit he was relieved when the door flew open. He ran in and put his back against their hallway wall while the friend peeked around in the hallway real fast and locked the door. He asked the friend for their phone so he could call his grandmother. He had to call twice before she answered, "Sapphire, that's you? Something bad is happening."

"Mama, it's me Mike. Listen and Listen well. The police are scouring the hall I got a way but I think Griff is dead."

"Oh, heaven no baby no," she interrupted and he listened briefly to her cries ready to break himself however he gained his composure.

"Mama, calm down. I need you to pay attention. You can tell them you drug Koi in the house but don't make no mention of me. They may search around a little bit but don't worry the house is free of drugs and I have my gun on me. You tell them I am out of town visiting relatives but you heard a young lady in the hallway screaming and when you looked out it was your friend's daughter so you drug her in. Don't worry, I will clean up all the blood and stuff but I think its best I lay low here for a while until it's safe to come home. Do you understand me mama?"

"Yes, baby loud and clear and Michael James Bracy," she said using his full name.

"Yes, mama," he respectfully answered.

"I love you and praying for your safe return home.

"I love you too mama. Don't you forget it. When I come home I am going to take you to the soul food restaurant you love so much in Harlem. You hear me my angel?" he asked his grandmother.

"Yes, baby. I hear you loud and clear." Mike hung up the phone and took a deep sigh of relief. He watched Sapphire as she returned from out the hallway with Griff's duffle bag full of money. She snuck to go get it while the cops called themselves securing the hallways and searching for suspects or more wounded victims.

"Damn, baby this is heavy. This is what six hundred grand feel like? Huh?" she asked Mike happily.

Mike eyed her and said, "Yes, now come over here and sit on my lap. I just want you to know that you are the only one I trust with this. I hope you don't do anything to break that trust."

"Baby don't worry. I am as loyal and faithful as they come. I am just glad that we finally got a big lick off this nigga. I was tired of messing up packages for pennies," she said seriously to Mike.

"Damn, I know but I didn't want him to die. He still was my boy but cheap as fuck. Sometimes you have to take what you need from who you need it from. You got me?"

Sapphire giggled and reached into the duffle bag grabbing bands of money. She imitated the 'Set it off' movie with Queen Latifah and said, "I got money."

Her and Mike cracked up laughing and then he reached for the money, grabbed it from her hands and placed it on the table. He kissed her neck and started telling her how beautiful, loyal and gangster she was to sneak and steal money after a shoot-out with the cops in close proximity. She batted her eyelashes and gave him an actress worthy line of, "I am, you don't say."

The two tongue kissed and then he told her to spread some of the money out so they could make love on top of it. They got into the groove and she pushed him on his back to put his beef stick in her mouth. It wasn't overly plump but it hit her spot and she was happy to finally have someone who went out of their way to please her.

After rolling around on the floor and her riding him for a minute they heard the front door of the apartment bang. Mike looked at her and said, "Now who the fuck could that be? If it's that bitch Kiki get rid of her."

Sapphire a little upset told him Kiki could wait her ass in the hallway until they bust their nuts. However, the door kept banging and being a little upset Sapphire yelled out, "Dang, who is it?"

The reply was enough to send them both reeling especially with the money spread out on the floor, "Ma'am it's the police open the door. We have some questions to ask you."

Frozen in fear, she turned around to look at Mike who already started scooping up the money to throw back in the bag. He whispered, "Stall them baby."

She talked to them through the door, "Officers I didn't call you."

"We know ma'am but there's been a shooting. Did you hear anything at all tonight?" they asked her.

"No, officer, I had my radio on and am just turning it off because it's late and my babies are sleeping," Sapphire lied to them. She didn't have the radio on nor did she have a child born from her hole in the world.

"Okay, ma'am do us one favor if you hear of anything or know of anything please do not hesitate to call us," and with that they left.

Sapphire returned to Mike and they re-spread the money out on the floor and continued with their lovemaking. The two thieves were oblivious to the fact Griff wasn't deceased and had one eye open watching Sapphire as she came and stole the bag of money. He vowed if he pulled through this to get the sweetest revenge on Mike and Sapphire, who were not only an item for a while now but he also suspected them of being the ones who were robbing his stash and messing up his packages. He was going to torture them both and make them beg for mercy. He would not be lenient on the wanna be 'Bonnie and Clyde' couple.

Griff's outlook on things was he was fair and lenient to his workers and homies. There was no need to rob him. As a result he was going to make them pay with every resource of torture he had available to him. He also wished for his little Shorty, his soldier, his rider to pull through it so she could get some payback herself. She was too good and loyal to fall to the schemes of the wicked. He was sorry for the things he put her through and hoped she lived through her injuries so he could make it up to her. He asked himself where were the EMT workers and at the same time heard them getting off the elevator with the cops not too far behind them.

As they were working on him, he mustered all the strength he had to tell them his friend was shot in an apartment. They asked him what door and he pointed to Mike's door and the cops went to investigate. Mike's Grandmother Marie opened up the door and explained to them she was nervous to look back out in the hallway once she dragged Koi in. The officers told her they understood and then they waved the second set of EMT's in to get started working on Koi.

They told Marie that Koi's pulse was low and that it was imperative they moved her now. They loaded her up on a gurney and hooked her up to a heart monitor when they heard her moaning. One of the technicians held their ear up to her mouth and heard her whispering a name, "Shaleeq." They then turned to Marie to ask her if there were a Shaleeq in the home.

Marie, taken aback said, "No sir. The only Shaleeq I know was her dad and he's been deceased for about nine years. Maybe she's delusional."

The emergency technician agreed and patted Koi's head, "Wow, she's just a baby. This is sad. Come on partner let's get her to Lincoln stat."

They headed for the door and Koi started pointing towards the door. "Yes, sweetie we are going to get you some help now and get you stabilized."

Koi shook her head back and forth real fast and her heart beat raced then she flat lined.

Marie started crying and begging God out loud to work a miracle for Koi. The EMT's raced for the door and Koi drifted into a state of Euphoria as her heart crashed. In her Euphoric state she saw Shaleeq and she called out crying, "Daddy, wait for me."

He turned around and stared at her. He told her to come on. The closer she got to him the more the heart monitor screeched indicating she was deceasing. She finally was upon Shaleeq and he wrapped his arms around her and his wings came out. She thought how beautiful her dad was as an angel and then he talked to her. He told her the importance of getting her respect back from Sapphire and Mike who tried to punk her and also getting his brother Mack to help her get the other children out of Foster care. He told her to find Angela and not fight with her but tell her the following message was from him; he forgave her for cheating on him with Mack and that he already knew the baby boy they had together wasn't his. She needs to make Mack take care of the whole clan more than what he was doing. Shaleeq told her there were more gems to be told, and hearts to mend, but for now that was it. He told her that he wanted nothing more than his princess with him but she was needed more on earth for her siblings and that she had to go back. Then he left her standing there bewildered.

The EMT's were elated when Koi's heart monitor started beeping. Although light, her pulse was back as well. They rushed her to Lincoln Hospital in one ambulance, and Griff in the other, hardly aware of their connection. They pulled up to the emergency room entrance and started racing towards triage but not after high fiving each other for a miraculous job. They lined Koi and Griff up next to each other who barely could keep their eyes open but managed a weak smile. They were then rushed into separate operating rooms where they remained for what seemed like forever to Marie, who found her way to the hospital for two reasons. One being she was genuinely concerned for Koi but also to keep Mike informed. She signed the papers for Koi as if she was her next of kin and could make any emergency health care decisions and then said to herself as she took a seat, "Let the waiting begin."

To be continued.........